# glitter

*A sparkling life well lived*

*A future cut too short*

*An impression never forgotten*

# Jennifer Anderson

Published by Insight International, Inc.
contact@freshword.com
www.freshword.com
918-493-1718

ISBN: 978-1-890900-95-3
E-book ISBN: 978-1-890900-01-4

Library of Congress Control Number: 2014956583

Printed in the United States of America.

# DEDICATION

This treasure is dedicated to my best friend and husband Joey and my beautiful, precious daughter Audrey. Both of you have given me the strength to move forward, the ground to stand on, and the oxygen to breathe. I could not have written this book without your support and enduring love. Until we can be reunited with our darling Lily, I will continue to live a "YES" with you.

# CONTENTS

# Introduction

I have prayed about it, and I felt my Lily pulling at my heart to do this book. She was a true inspiration to so many, so by writing her story and including how she has changed so many lives, I feel that I am doing my job here on earth. If you had asked me five years ago where I saw myself, I can assure you that writing a book would not be on my list! But sometimes God has different plans for us, and we have to be able to switch gears even when it is uncomfortable.

That is exactly what happened when Lily was diagnosed with cancer. I will *never* forget my husband picking me up off the floor of the hospital and saying, "You quit, she quits! You fight, she fights!"

Lily lived longer than all of the doctors expected because we didn't quit! God used Lily in so many ways, and I can only share so many of them with you in this book. I know there are people all over suffering with disease, sorrow, depression, and loss. But maybe reading a book about my little girl, who lived a "YES" life, will change something in you. Maybe it will inspire you to not give up or throw in the towel.

My hope and prayer are that in reading her story, you too will be inspired to choose to live a "YES" with your life!

glitter

*Lily.*

# 1

# Living a "YES" Life

**Glitter:** *An assortment of very small, flat, reflective particles. When particles are applied to surfaces, they reflect light at different angles, causing the surface to sparkle or shimmer.*[1] If you've ever played with glitter, you know it gets everywhere—it even sticks to you.

It may sound odd to you when you first hear it, but the definition for "glitter" describes my daughter Lily perfectly! Small and bright, she reflected the light inside her, and she sparkled and shimmered wherever she went. But she didn't just glitter when she was present—she sparkled long after she left a room, sticking with people. The light she reflected to the people she touched endures, even though my Lily has gone up to be with the Father of all lights.

The thing that made Lily stand out and let her light "stick" with people was that she lived what we call a "YES Life." Even as a young child, people would stop to comment on something special they saw in Lily. "She's so pretty," they'd say. "There's just something about her...." She would give people these amazing

---

[1] http://en.wikipedia.org/wiki/Glitter.

hugs—she would dive in, not caring if she only came up to your kneecap, and would wrap around people to give full-body hugs.

This was when she was little—two or three. At the time, I didn't realize how special she was, but now I can look back and see that she was like an angel on assignment to earth. Her presence made a difference to people—those who knew her well, and those she didn't even meet.

My little girl battled an evil monster called cancer to a stand-still for three-and-a-half years, exceeding every expectation and beating the odds. And despite brutal treatments and enduring difficulties absolutely no kid should *ever* endure, Lily still shone. Her smile still warmed hearts. Her laughter still brought music to people's ears.

During her eleven years and 203 days on earth, Lily brought a special gift of light and optimism that inspired literally thousands upon thousands of people. It left a standard for me to follow, a call to something more than wishful thinking and bigger than simple optimism.

Lily embodied "YES" living. She lived "YES" with her every breath, and when she no longer breathed, she left the rest of us seeking for more "YES" in our own lives.

That's why I wrote this book. The world needs more "YES!" in it! And if Lily's story can help us reach for it, if she can inspire more "YES" living, then her glitter will stick to lives far longer than she could have ever lived.

*That* is what she would have wanted—to know that her time here had inspired others to choose to live a "YES" life. That's my goal and my challenge to you, readers. When you're done reading her story, you will mourn with us that the world is a little dimmer without her, but you will come away sticky with light and life!

When you're done reading, my hope is that you have Lily glitter all over you!

## Living a Miracle

What do you do when you are handed the absolute worst news you could ever hear?

When the doctor told me that my child had cancer, I literally felt the breath knocked out of me by the impact of those words. I slid down a hospital wall with no strength in my legs, and darkness spreading over my mind.

A cancer diagnosis is something I would not wish on anyone. It is a truly terrible thing. But a cancer diagnosis for your *child* is something that will take you through the valley of the shadow of death. It will push your entire family to the end of its strength, and it will simultaneously break your heart and give you a super-human capacity to endure.

I've heard from so many people that Lily inspired them. With her courage, her positive attitude, and the special light that seemed to shine out from those beautiful hazel eyes, she moved people to make positive decisions and take positive action.

Our pastor, Steven Gibbs, described it best when he said that Lily lived a "YES" life. She chose, incredibly, to be cheerful throughout a very difficult and painful disease. She chose to study hard in school and celebrate her friends' accomplishments even when she could no longer participate. She chose to reach out to others and expect the best, even though she could have shut down and given up. Amazingly, her small choices every day had a ripple effect I could not have imagined, and I still get letters today from people I have never met who were touched by Lily's story.

Lily lived with us for eleven years on this earth. She spent three of those years in the fight of her life against Stage 4 neuroblastoma—and kicked its butt over and over again. Ultimately, she escaped cancer's reach altogether when God brought her home to heaven. In her eleven short years, Lily touched thousands of lives with her unique spark and passion. Through our cancer journey, she traveled the country, met and sang to celebrities, flew in private jets, and sang the National Anthem on big stages. Lily was also the first child in the U.S. to receive FDA approval for a new experimental cancer treatment drug.

She experienced some big things, and those are very special memories now. Even more precious, though, are the everyday memories. The goofy ones when Lily and little sister Audrey played dress-up and dolls and fussed at each other in the morning. The tender ones, like when my husband gently explained the concept of death to our small daughter one night at bedtime and all the nights I crawled into Lily's bed to spoon her and hold her tight. And the transcendent ones, when I know God came down very near to comfort and give one more day of strength to my brave girl.

On the face of it, our story doesn't have a "happy" ending. It surely doesn't have the one that I would have chosen for us. However, looking back, I can see that even though she died, Lily still left us a miracle. Her *life* was the miracle.

Though I don't have Lily here with me, I have such a legacy. Lily's legacy of "YES" living inspires me to be stronger, better, and braver—no matter what I'm facing. She inspired thousands of other people to live life more fully. Somehow, she just…shined, and everyone who met her could see that light.

At the end of her fight, Lily saw heaven. I know that she is there now, healthy and whole and probably talking God's ear off about something to do with fashion and the angels' attire.

Lily Anderson is my daughter, but she is more than that. She is my inspiration and my hero—she glittered with a light reflected from the Source of all lights. I hope you will be inspired by her life as well and choose to live a "YES" life every single day.

## Meet the Andersons

*Meet the Andersons! Left to Right: Audrey, Jennifer, Lily and Joey—go, Anderson Power!*

Joey and I married back in 2000, and Lily was born just a year later in May 2001. It was a perfect pregnancy, perfect delivery, a beautiful baby girl. For five years, she was our only child.

We were living in Atlanta. My husband's custom cabinetry business was booming, and I was selling real estate and loved it. It was a great time—two incomes, a happy home, and a little baby girl.

The only thing that could make it better was the arrival of our Audrey in February 2007. My friend picked Lily up early from kindergarten that day, and brought her to the hospital to meet her baby sister. Lily came into the hospital room wearing her little skirt and sweater, Mary Jane shoes, and braids...even then she was a fashionista! She was grinning from ear to ear and brought in a little stuffed animal to give to Audrey. It was love at first sight for big sister (although Lily had to get used to sharing Mommy with this new little person)!

Looking back, our life was good but a little...unaware. We were both working full time, home at 6 o'clock, "Hi Honey, how was your day?" and have some dinner. We moved into a bigger house in the neighborhood shortly after Audrey was born, and our wonderful nanny Nancy (who is still with us) cared for Audrey and Lily during the day. The Anderson train was moving along at a nice brisk pace, and I didn't even notice how fast we were going. Life was busy and very full, and we didn't really slow down for the next two years.

But in 2009, we received the diagnosis that derailed our train completely.

# 2

# It's Not Stomach Trouble

In February of 2009, Lily started complaining of stomach trouble. She was up at night crying and saying her stomach hurt, so I took her to the emergency room at the hospital close to our house. The doctors there did x-rays and took blood, and said that she simply had gas.

When they looked at the x-rays, I remember the doctor saying, "Do you see this right here?" He had the x-ray up on a light, and pointed out her liver in a place he didn't expect it to be. However, he reassured me it was caused by the way Lily was laying for the x-ray and was no cause for concern.

That night we went home and stocked up on all the gas medicines at the store. It was inconvenient, but no big deal. And honestly, gas is one of those things you have to laugh at, especially at eight years old. Joey, Lily, and Audrey all think that "toots," as they call them, are hilarious. I don't know what it is about boys and tooting, but I just had to shake my head that my precious little ladies thought that gas was so funny! So Lily and Joey found it hysterical that we'd gone in and found out that "toots" were her problem.

So, Lily had "gas." She took her medicine, and we gave her extra fiber to help her go to the bathroom. Her stomach pain faded and flared occasionally, but mostly it was just one of those things you live with. Crohn's disease and irritable bowel syndrome run in our family; honestly, I was thrilled it was gas. No problem—we could manage *that*.

We went on vacation that summer to the beach with a couple of other families. The pain flared up again but Lily, trouper that she was, fought through. There was no way she was going to miss the beach and all the fun with her friends, so we powered through and kept on going.

However, in September 2009, Lily had really severe stomach pain. This time I took her to her own pediatrician for an exam. Dr. Munshi took blood samples and said she would call back with the results. Two hours later, the doctor called and said, "We need you to take her to the emergency room immediately. Her CRP number [which is a protein in your blood] is higher than any number we've ever seen before. We've never seen this before, and it indicates inflammation in her body."

## Every Parent's Nightmare

I will never forget getting that call from the pediatrician. Joey was out of town. I was by myself with Lily, and I had somebody take Audrey for the day so we could get to the hospital. It was a Saturday, and the Georgia Bulldogs were playing.

My friend Heidi insisted on coming with us even though she was having a game day party and hosting thirty people at her house. I tried to tell her not to leave her friends and party; I wasn't worried about what we would learn here and told her we were fine. She came anyway. I'm so thankful she did. Heidi was a faithful friend through thick and thin for me, and her daughter, Sophie, was Lily's true best friend since they met in preschool.

We had to wait around forever, wearing masks because Swine Flu was just recently on the scene. First, they did an X-ray. "Mommy," Lily kept asking, "is everything okay? Am I going to be okay?" She wondered why everyone was wearing masks, which made us both hot as we breathed through them. My anxiety level kept rising. Within two hours they had already done a CT scan. Shortly after, Dr. Ramey came into our room with a somber face. By this time, Lily had fallen asleep, and I left her with Heidi as I stepped out with the doctor.

Dr. Ramey, who was nine month's pregnant, was very kind as she gently said, "We know why Lily is having stomach pains. We found a tumor."

With those words, the whole world slowed down to a dead stop. I felt like we were in a movie scene. I lost control of my limbs and my voice, and I remember sliding against the wall to the floor in a haze.

I couldn't speak—so I screamed. "Is it cancer?" The world had stopped spinning for me; my entire focus was telescoping down on the words I could not imagine hearing next.

Dr. Ramey continued in the same calm, kind voice. "We see a mass on the CT scan. We think it's cancer."

I was already on the floor. I couldn't breathe. Then, screaming, all I could think was, *IS SHE GOING TO DIE?*

I will never forget Dr. Ramey looking at me and saying firmly, "No."

This answer was a blessing. She could have said, "I don't know." She could have said, "The test results don't look good." But she said, "No"—and she meant it, and in that moment she saved me from falling over the abyss.

But I just couldn't take it—a moment later, I started dry heaving in the trash. My mind and my body were rejecting this awful moment, but I knew in some part of me that I had to face it and act. I knew the first thing I had to do was call Joey and tell him.

Joey was probably two hours away, but somehow he was at the hospital within forty-five minutes. Immediately, his analytical nature kicked in. Heidi had called and left him a message, but it was almost like he didn't believe it. He wanted the doctor to explain it to him personally, and Dr. Ramey had to go over it again with him. He started asking questions: What kind of tumor is it? How big is it? Where is the tumor in her body?

Dr. Ramey's answer floored me again. "Yes, there's a mass inside her, and it's behind her liver." As Joey heard answers, he began to fall apart, his head in his hands.

I flashed back to that moment in the ER months before, when the x-ray showed her liver where it shouldn't have been. Her liver has been pushed into the x-ray. Had the tumor been there even then? Dr. Ramey told us that the tumor was big, as big a bowling ball, but flat and it was pushing her liver down.

They didn't know it yet, but Lily's cancer was called neuroblastoma. It is typically found at Stage 4, usually in the form of a tumor like Lily had around the adrenal glands. It's usually found in the bones, the bone marrow, and by the time they find it, it's everywhere. When they found Lily's tumor, it was huge; it had already spread to her bones and her bone marrow.

# The Fight Begins

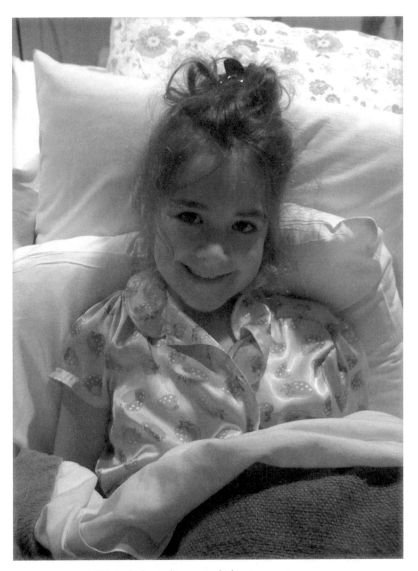

*Lily in the hospital just a couple days into our journey...*

By the time it had all sunk in, as much as it could, it was past midnight. We were taken immediately to the Aflac Cancer Center in the hospital and admitted. I'll never forget walking by a sign on the wall that said "Aflac Cancer Center and Blood Disorder." All I could think is, *What are we doing here?*

Once admitted, it all came rushing at us, wave upon wave. We met with doctors. We met with nurses. We met with oncologists and specialists to get the treatment plan into action immediately. Joey and I did our best to keep our wits about us as people in white coats rushed and bustled in and out.

Thankfully, Lily was sleeping during all this craziness. I feared the morning…how would I tell this? *How on earth are we going to tell her this?*

That first night, between meetings with doctors, we started calling family. Of course, it was the middle of the night. Normal people are sleeping! I called my mom; no answer. I called my dad; no answer. I called my brother out-of-state and told him, "Lily has cancer. You need to get hold of Mom and Dad!" The only way he could reach them was to call the police and have them go bang on the door at three in the morning! They all lived hours away, but by 7 o'clock in the morning my entire family was standing in the hospital.

That was September 5, 2009, and Lily was eight years old. We went in for simple stomach pain and gas, never expecting that the hospital and staff would become our second home on and off for the next three-and-a-half years.

## 3

# From Sixty-nine to Forty-two

The next morning, it was time to give Lily her diagnosis. She knew she was sick and that something was wrong, and she waited with serious eyes as the hospital staff walked in. The children's hospital has what they call Child Life Specialists, and they are there to explain things to the children in a way they can understand. Thank goodness they do!

I was shaking. "How am I going to tell her this? How am I going to tell her this?"

They said, "That's our job." And they did an amazing job of doing what I knew I could not.

The Child Life Specialist came in with a model of a child and explained to Lily everything that was going to happen to her. The doll had what's called a central line. It had a port in the chest with two lines coming out of it for medicine, so chemotherapy can go into the tubes.

She showed Lily on the doll and explained, "Lily, you're going to have surgery, and the first surgery you're going to have you're going to be put to sleep. They're going to cut your tummy a little bit and take a sample of the tumor because they want to figure out what kind it is."

The specialist continued in her explanation to Lily, and Lily listened and nodded with a composure that stunned me. Pointing to the doll, the specialist explained the medicine would go up into the line. Lily would have a port put in during the surgery. When she woke up, she would have two lines coming out of her chest. When the medicine went in, Lily was warned that she might feel yucky.

In fact, she might feel very yucky. She might throw up. Mommy and Daddy would be with her, and the hospital would give her nausea medicine. The specialist told every detail about what was going to happen, and then she said, "And then sometimes when you take this medicine, your hair falls out."

Lily's beautiful, thick curly brown hair came halfway down her back. She was proud of her hair and so fashion-conscious that her nickname was "Style"—Style Anderson.

(I actually gave her this nickname later, after she had already been fighting cancer. We were getting ready to go somewhere when she came into my bathroom and asked me, "Are you wearing that?" I looked at my outfit. "Well, I *was*... I guess I," I said hesitantly. "Am I the only one in this family who has style?" Lily asked, exasperated. Yep, "Style" Anderson—it was a perfect fit for her.)

I imagined my beautiful girl—sick and bald with cancer, with lines coming out of her chest.... I thought I couldn't fall further into the darkness, but this was almost too much. My little fashionista, who could put an adorable outfit together in minutes that would have her friends commenting on it, who always knew exactly what to do with her hair....

She asked, "I'm going to lose my hair?"

The specialist replied, "Sometimes you lose your hair."

Then Lily said, "That's okay. It'll grow back." Simple as that: "It'll grow back." A smile and a shrug. She was eight, and she was taking this news without a moment of fear.

Looking at her, I realized, *She's right.* Of course she's right, and it will grow back, and it's not worth the time and energy to worry over it.

Looking back to that moment, I can see that it set the stage for how Lily chose to deal with her illness. Not just the hair loss, but the physical pain, the loss of a normal childhood routine, the separation and isolation from her friends and family. Somehow, Lily saw past it to the goal, and the goal was to beat cancer...period. Her giant determination, set inside her small body, was impressive. You could take one look at her beautiful face and instantly know there was no stopping her! This was Lily, without even realizing it, choosing the "Yes life" of hope and confidence...while the doctors talked about chemo and ports and throwing up.

## Surgery

Lily's surgery was on September 11th, which also was our wedding anniversary. Frankly, I would have picked almost any other way to spend that day! But, there we were and we were blessed to have the most amazing, unbelievably kind surgeon. Her name was Dr. Julie Glasson. She and the nurse, also named Julie, greeted Lily for surgery with a tiara and a wand, and Dr. Glasson told us, "Everything's going to be okay."

The biopsy surgery left a seven-inch incision across her abdomen, which was painful for Lily, and she had her port placed on the left side of her chest. One line connected directly to a vein close to Lily's heart, and the other connected to a main artery to spread medicine through the whole body.

Even though we were still waiting the results of the biopsy, the hospital was treating the tumor aggressively due to its large size and quick growth. Normally a port is under the skin and can be accessed with just a needle. In Lily's case, it was so serious the doctors had to be able to administer fluids and chemotherapy at the same time. The chemo was so toxic, they had to administer fluids at the same time to keep it from burning her. So Lily had two lines coming out of her chest, just as the Child Life Specialist had explained, and she had her first chemotherapy the next day.

When Lily went into the hospital on September 5th, she weighed sixty-nine pounds. After her first chemo, she got really sick, really fast. The chemo is supposed to take your blood counts down, and your body is supposed to make more. For Lily, though, the cancer was also in her bone marrow, which is what *makes* the new blood. A child's normal hemoglobin count might be fourteen or fifteen; Lily's was down to a six. It took her little body a long time to come back from that first treatment; we were in the hospital for twenty-two days, and in that time, Lily lost *twenty-seven pounds*. In that short time, Lily went from wearing a size eight to wearing a size five. Audrey was almost three at the time, and I'll never forget having to bring Audrey's underwear to the hospital so Lily could put them on.

I could not believe we had gone from, "Mommy, my tummy hurts," to being so sick, sick, *sick* that my baby weighed only forty-two pounds. You could see her little bones. That was hard, but so was seeing her hair as it fell out, dark and easy to see against her white pillow cover several weeks later after we were back home.

## The Enemy Gets a Name

Lily's chemo treatments were on a twenty-one day cycle, meaning that she would have the first treatment, wait three weeks, and go back for the next one. Before that, though, the final biopsy test came in and we heard the official diagnosis for the first time: Stage 4 neuroblastoma.

(Neuroblastoma? I've heard of leukemia, but seriously…what kind of weird cancer was this?!)

As the doctors explained, neuroblastoma is a type of cancer normally found in infants and rarely in children over ten, and it's usually little boys. So I had an eight-year-old girl with neuroblastoma. They said that Lily was born with the gene and that something in her was not able to fight it off.

I can't explain the fear the moment when I heard the name of the monster inside my baby's body. I sagged down the wall, unable to support myself. When they said, "Stage 4," I asked, "What's Stage 5?" I didn't know that there *is* no Stage 5. Stage 4 is the worst case, and I fell apart again at this awful new knowledge.

Then, maybe because they didn't want me making a scene in the hallway, they pulled Joey and me into a conference room. The doctor sat down and told us what we were facing. He gave us the statistics—numbers I didn't want to hear. "I don't want to hear how many kids do what," I told him. I choked out, "She's going to be okay."

I didn't listen after that—I was freaking out. Joey had to tell me. It was bad. Children with neuroblastoma have just a 50 percent chance of survival. But in Lily's case, the tumor was encapsulating her kidney and the cancer had spread to her lung, her spine, the bones in her arm and skull, and her bone marrow. According to the doctor, Lily had just six months to live.

## We're Going to Be in the 50 Percent

I remember Joey and I looked at each other, and we knew…we knew instantly that no matter what the statistics said, Lily was going to live. When we heard 50 percent, we decided that Lily would be one of them who made it, no matter what it took or what we had to do. She would survive, and we were going to beat this.

Joey remained so calm, so positive. "Somebody is in that 50 percent," he would say. "Lily is going to be in that 50 percent." He would remind me constantly that we were going to be in that half that made it. If she had a 10 percent chance, he would've said that she would be that one in ten who made it.

We didn't tell Lily. She didn't need to know about the odds stacked against her; she had enough to handle. We told her that she was sick—very sick. "It's something called 'cancer,'" we told her. "Treatment takes a year-and-a-half—but after that we're going to be good."

Lily was a smart little girl, but she was still young—she listened to her mom. If she were a teenager, she might have said we were lying. But we were telling her what we believed. The doctors may not have thought she'd even make it through the chemo, but we were not going to accept it. We would still be here in a year-and-a-half, we vowed—we would *all* still be here, because we were fighting to win!

## Climb That Mountain

Those days are a whirlwind in my memory now, but a couple of chance meetings are vivid to this day.

On Lily's third day in the hospital, I hit a real low and began to cry in the hallway. I was having trouble breathing because I'd been crying so much. I was walking with my cousin Erin.

Out of nowhere, a beautiful, larger-than-life African-American woman appeared and started to scold me. She got into my face: "You stop crying. You need to stop crying. Your daughter needs you. You climb that mountain. You take down that mountain. You cry no *more*."

I remember her saying, "You cry no more, you climb that mountain," and then she left. I looked for her after that, sure I would see her somewhere at the hospital, sure she must have been there for some reason. I never saw her again. I've since wondered if she was some kind of divine vision, but I know for sure that whether she was heavenly or earthly, she was an angel to me that day.

Even though we had an "angel" come visit us, not everything we heard was positive. We had to be careful about what we let in. Some people had been battered by their experiences and did not have the same attitude we held. We wanted to tackle our challenge with optimism, and we had absolutely, completely *zero* room for negativity in our hospital room! I wasn't going to let it go anywhere near Lily. We were choosing a "YES" life, and nobody was going to distract us from the goal.

## 4

# Anderson Power!

During all this craziness, my whole outside world just stopped. I wasn't a real estate agent or anything else anymore...I was just a mom, and I couldn't bear to leave Lily's side. However, there really wasn't a way for Joey to do that. Joey and a partner had a custom cabinet shop, and he had to be there.

I remember looking at him and talking about how we were going to do this. I said, "You've got to keep normalcy in our family, because Lily needs to know that we're not freaking out. If Daddy is going to work and I'm taking care of her, everything feels fine. But if you're home with me or sitting in this hospital room, and we're both looking at each other like deer in headlights, she's going to know that there's a real problem." And there was a problem. We knew that this was scary, but we didn't want Lily or Audrey to be scared. We didn't want them to feel it.

So Joey went back to work and would come see Lily after work. After staying those first scary days with our dear friends Wendy and Doug, Audrey came home, too. She and Joey started on our new normal at home...while Lily and I navigated online school and oxygen tanks at the hospital. I didn't leave her side—for the entire time we were there, we were together.

Nancy, our nanny of over two years, took care of Audrey during the day, and my mom was at the hospital with me (by that time the rest of my family had gone home, though they would come visit when they could).

Before all this, I never thought about how cancer can affect an entire family. Divorce is unfortunately quite common, and it's easy to understand why. The cancer takes so much of your focus that almost everything else moves to the back burner. This is especially hard if you have other children at home—you are physically separated from them for long periods, to say nothing of the impact on your marriage. The stress of it all can be crushing. I remember seeing a husband and wife get into an actual fistfight in the hospital hallway, fighting about some mundane thing as their child fought for life in their hospital room.

That was another reason Joey and I protected our normalcy...not only for our girls but for ourselves. We had to remember each other. We purposed to give each other grace and tried very hard to understand each other better. We realized we were in a situation where the little things needed a lot of grace and where things like whether we washed the car today or tomorrow weren't worth an argument.

Lily often told us, "Things happen for a reason." I believe that...although I realize that I will have to wait to get to heaven to understand the full reason for Lily's illness. "Well, Mom, things happen for a reason," she would say with a smile and maybe an eye roll for whatever was causing the trouble.

That's Lily—she got a lot of her common sense from her dad. Joey is very strong, levelheaded, and very smart.

I remember crying hysterically one day, and I said, "I don't know how to do this. This is just so hard." Joey looked at me and said, "Jennifer, we signed up for *hard*. We signed up for it." He's right. When I got married and decided to have children, I signed up for hard. That's not easy. He said, "We signed up for hard. You going to quit?" I wasn't—ever.

We were up against a nightmare, and that's all he had to say to me: "We signed up for hard." Really, as a parent, there isn't any other choice. You have to just keep fighting, keep moving forward. We would never quit.

Joey is the one who came up with our family cheer, too. People have heard us say, "Anderson Power!" and we often reminded each other of Anderson Power during Lily's journey. It was something he taught the girls when they were very little—at bath time. He'd say, "Lily, Audrey, you guys can do anything because you have Anderson Power," and they even made up the song to go with it.

When Joey gave them a bath, he came up with the "Anderson Power" cheer to get them to wash their hair—both girls hated washing their hair! He'd say, "You've got to lean…" and they'd flex their muscles "…mean…" they'd make a mean face "…and *clean!*" and then he'd scrub their hair. It was the only way that he could get them to wash their hair!

The girls would be in the tub, and Joey would say, "You can do anything because you have Anderson Power. You can be mean and lean and clean!" He'd wash their hair as they sang their song.

Anderson Power became our motto. We leaned on that power, we leaned on each other, and we held each other up.

Throughout my family's cancer journey, many people said, "I don't know how you do this. I could never do it!"

The truth is, you could do it if you had to. You would do anything and everything you had to do if it was your child. You find the strength because...what's the alternative? Giving up? That's not a choice! You fight, and you research, and you ask questions, and you bombard heaven with prayers. And then, at the end of your strength...you trust. You trust the surgeons to skillfully do their job, and you trust the Lord with all the things you cannot control.

Joey is my rock. He said many times during my low moments, "Jennifer, if we fight, Lily fights. If we quit, she quits."

Quitting is not an option for us. Anderson Power!

# 5

# Coming Home

After nearly a month in the hospital—and Lily's first round of chemotherapy—we were finally able to bring her home. It had been a very difficult process, made worse by the fact that every time we thought we were ready to go home, Lily would get a fever. Now, when you have a port and cancer like Lily had, if you have a fever, you can't go home. She had to be without fever for 48 hours before they'd release us, and she kept getting fevers in the middle of the night. Some were as high as 104, others were 100.

Finally she had made it 24 hours without a fever and I started to get excited. *This is going to be the day,* I thought. They even told us they were going to let us go home.

We were home two hours—*two hours!*—and her fever was back. I had to call the hospital and tell them. "We just cleaned your room," they told me. "You can have it right back—bring her back." We had to stay a couple more days, but finally we went long enough without a fever to head home again!

Lily was so excited, and as we turned down the street into our neighborhood, we were all surprised to see the trees decorated with lime green bows and ribbons all the way down the street!

Lily's favorite colors were pink and green, and our neighbors and friends were welcoming Lily home!

Audrey had missed her big sister terribly. She ran to Lily and gave her about twenty kisses before letting her go, and Lily held onto her baby sister and just squeezed her. It blessed my heart to see them back together...but I really knew I was home again when I heard them bickering over something in Lily's room the next day! Never has childhood fussing sounded so sweet; it meant that Lily had enough energy to fight.

Five years apart in age, Audrey and Lily adored each other but of course squabbled as all sisters do. Joey had the perfect advice for Lily on how to deal with her baby sister. Whenever eight-year-old Lily would get frustrated about something two-and-a-half-year-old Audrey had done, Joey would remind her, "Lillian, you simply can't reason with someone who poops her pants. Why are you trying to reason with someone who poops her pants?" Somehow, that simple advice always smoothed away the conflict (and made me laugh—every time!)

Another memory that still makes me laugh today was the "spaghetti incident" that happened the second night we were home from the hospital. Lily wasn't very hungry but thought she could eat some pasta. If you've ever known someone going through chemo, then you know that it destroys any appetite for food in addition to the nausea it causes. By this point, Lily's little body was frail from weight loss, so when she said she could eat some pasta, I got spaghetti to the table as quickly as humanly possible. The four of us sat down to dinner just like normal, and Lily ate several big bites. Then suddenly, she heaved and threw it all back up again.

Amazingly, the noodles came out of Lily looking almost untouched, and landed in a perfect arc right back in Lily's bowl! We all sat in surprised silence for a moment, looking at that bowl of noodles. Audrey looked at the bowl, then looked at me, and asked with concern, "Lily no like 'sketti?" She didn't understand the explosion of laughter that followed, but joined in with us anyway.

If Lily was my hero, I have to say that Audrey is my sunshine. Even at that young age, Audrey's instinct was to make us laugh and encourage Lily. I remember the very first time I had to change the dressing on Lily's port at home. It was awful. The bandage tape had caused some kind of allergic reaction, and it tore Lily's skin as I tried to remove it. We were upstairs, and Lily was screaming in pain for an hour as I tried to remove the old dressing slowly and gently without ripping Lily's delicate skin.

After what felt like forever, we finally got the dressing changed, and came back downstairs. Audrey had heard Lily's cries and had been waiting. As soon as she saw her sister, Audrey burst into a cheer. She was so little, she couldn't pronounce her L's—so "Let's go Lily!" came out "Wets go Wiwwy!" Hearing her shriek her sister's name in such utter joy will stay with me forever.

## Lily's Run

While Joey and I were trying to maintain "normal" at home, our friends and neighbors were doing something extraordinary. They had mobilized to take care of my family by bringing food to the house every day, and almost as soon as we received Lily's diagnosis, they began to raise money to cover her medical expenses. One dear friend arranged a Mary Kay party, and another arranged a golf tournament. Our friends rallied together to help us put on a 5K race and fun run.

Somehow, in less than a month's time, we put together the first annual "Lily's Run" on October 11, 2009, with the help of Kingdom Kids, a really wonderful organization. We had hoped for at least 200 registrants but had 350 race bibs ready to go. However, no one was prepared for the overwhelming response. All 350 race numbers sold out early on race day, and hundreds more runners lined up with no number. I think we had nearly a thousand runners total that day! Some knew us personally, but many came simply because they were inspired by Lily's story. In fact, the winner didn't even get a bib—and he turned out to be her oncologist's son!

There had been several local news stories about the race by this point, and newspaper and television crews to talk about her diagnosis and treatment had interviewed Lily. She was tired and weak, but she got to ride on a fire truck that came to pick us up— and I have to say she enjoyed every minute. She loved the opportunity to be on television, and she was truly excited to realize how many people were supporting her in her recovery.

That first "Lily's Run" turned out to be an absolutely amazing day. In addition to the run, there was a craft booth to make Lily necklaces, a pumpkin patch, a bake sale, inflatables, and a silent auction. Restaurants donated delicious food, a local florist brought lilies to give away for donations, and generous individuals donated their time to do face painting and make balloon animals. A band played, and the school cheerleaders encouraged runners along the route.

The race came during Lily's second round of chemo, and she was feeling very sick from the treatment. Since her immune system was so low, we didn't want her at the beginning of the race around so many people. However, she insisted on waiting at the halfway point, and she waved and shouted thank yous as each of the one thousand runners passed her. In her bright green shirt, a lime green bandana covering her head, Lily's huge smile relayed her joy and gratitude to all her new friends.

The highlight of the day was when Lily took the microphone to sing *The Climb* by Miley Cyrus—sick and skinny, she just sang her heart out...while Joey and I bawled.

Lily loved this song and found strength in the lyrics. It talks about all the struggles we face. She loved the way the song described there always being more mountains in our way as we fight an uphill battle. One line from the song goes, *"Ain't about how fast I get there, ain't about what's waiting on the other side. It's the climb."* You can see why this was her theme song!

## Stem Cells

The day after "Lily's Run," we drove to Memphis to have Lily's stem cells harvested at St. Jude Children's Hospital because we couldn't get our insurance to cover her procedure where we lived in Atlanta. We desperately wanted to stay in Atlanta, and I went banging on doors for a spot contract so we could be treated in Atlanta. But because of an insurance issue, we had to pick from an approved list of hospitals—and that meant traveling to St. Jude Hospital in Memphis, Tennessee.

The crazy thing is, as hard as it was to travel with two-year-old Audrey and Lily, who was fighting cancer, it ended up being a blessing. St. Jude is an incredible place—it's the mecca for children fighting cancer. It is truly state-of-the-art, world-class, and impeccably sterile. The hospital is funded entirely by charitable donations, and no child ever has to pay to come there for treatment. If you ever see those commercials on TV for St. Jude's and wonder where your money goes, I can personally say that it is going to a truly wonderful place—and is money well spent. We were there a week waiting for Lily's blood counts to be just right for the procedure, and we were completely impressed by the whole hospital and staff.

The stem cell harvesting procedure was fascinating, albeit a bit scary from a mother's perspective. A line would have to be surgically inserted in her groin area to draw the blood out. Lily was confined to bed for six hours with nothing to eat or drink while her body's entire supply of blood cycled through. All she could do was lie in bed and watch movies. Joey and I pulled our chairs as close to her bed as we could, and we all watched movies together until the process was complete. The machine would spin her blood to separate out the stem cells, and the rest of her blood would be returned to her body. Stem cells would help make healthy blood, but her body had to be cancer-free first.

The goal of the procedure was to harvest as many stem cells as possible, freeze them, and then later return them to Lily's body once the chemo treatments had removed all the cancer from her bone marrow. Stem cells are "baby cells"; they can become literally any kind of cell in the body as they mature. They can grow into skin cells, or muscle cells, or liver cells. If cancer is present, they might join the gang and become cancer cells. However, Lily's stem cells were going to be saved until all those bad cells were gone. Then we would return to St. Jude, and they would transplant

Lily's own stem cells back into her body. Those stem cells could go to work making new, healthy bone marrow cells, which would in turn make new, healthy blood.

It sometimes takes a few days to get enough stem cells from a child's bloodstream, but not our Lily. She wanted to go home, so her little body made millions—we got them on the first day.

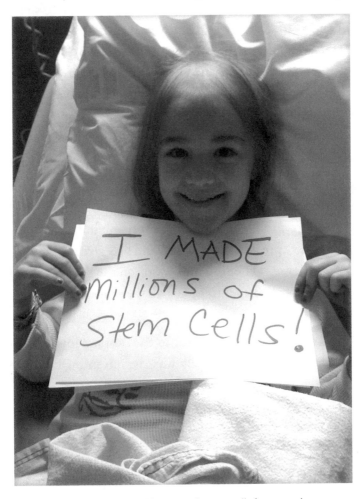

*Lily at St. Jude Hospital harvesting her stem cells for a transplant.*

By this point, Lily didn't like hospitals. Who could blame her? But she was so nice to the doctors and nurses—and so full of questions! She wanted to know everything: "What are we going to do next?" or, "Is this going to hurt?" She was constantly comparing what they did to how they did it back at home, and she wanted to know why they were doing it differently.

But my favorite of her questions was just flat out asking, "Are you qualified to do this? Do you have a license? Did you study this?" She asked this of her oncologist at St. Jude, Dr. Triplett—who was as bald as she was by now! They made quite the pair, the bald twins, and she loved Dr. Triplett. And that was Lily—she made friends everywhere she went with her infectious "YES" attitude, and those she met couldn't help but be touched by it.

We returned from Memphis that weekend: in time for Lily to walk the field as Homecoming Queen for the West Forsyth Wolverines. She was so excited! She was escorted across the field by Joey, Audrey, and me...and loved every minute of being in the spotlight. She wore a beautiful dress and was given a crown and a bouquet of flowers. Then, all of the kids on the field released lime green balloons into the air to signify all the prayers that were going out for her.

On Monday, it would be back to the hospital for a scheduled bone scan. But for that day, Lily was the queen for many loving supporters as she was for us every day.

## Living in Two Worlds

Looking back at that time, I remember Lily moving almost effortlessly between her hospital world and her normal world.

Understand, between the time we learned she was sick and had the stem cell procedure was only about a month and a half—she still very much wanted to go right on living her "YES" life even when it was interrupted by hospital visits.

While in the hospital for treatments, she would panic about falling behind in her school work and would to go down to the hospital school for lessons (she loved learning and didn't want to fall behind in class). She sang and performed for the hospital staff, and she always lit up the dreary hallways with her giggles and spark. When she was home, we had to keep her isolated from school and friends because of the risk of germs and infection. But that didn't stop her from short visits with close friends, air kisses, waves instead of hugs, and long, girlish chats on the phone. She missed her class field trip to a local gem mine, but her dear friend Sophie brought her back a beautiful stone and a little bracelet and told her all about it.

Of course Lily got irritated and cranky about things along the way, but she never resented the things she didn't have. When her hair began to fall out from the chemo, she met with a wonderful wig maker who helped her pick exactly the right color hair and helped her style it just like Selena Gomez. Although she wasn't able to be at school with her friends, she delighted in hearing all about their days and the goings-on in class. When total strangers would stare at her smooth bald head, she would just twinkle back from behind her protective face mask and keep on going. When the local newspaper asked about her cancer, she rolled her eyes with a laugh and said she had to beat it quickly so she could get back to her singing and cheerleading.

# glitter

I've always said that Lily was an angel. She didn't always act like one, but I think that was just her cover.

6

# American Girl Getaway

About this time, something truly amazing happened that I have to share. One day, I got a call from Debbie Kalb. Debbie is a very special friend and is a Royal Black Diamond in the MonaVie business. She called to ask if Lily and I could attend an American Girl Doll fashion show and tea party the following week in Orlando. I was stunned by her generosity and thrilled at the thought, but wondered if Lily could safely travel on a commercial flight. I told Debbie we'd love to go, but I would have to check with the doctor first.

We started checking on flights and considering the risks, when Debbie called back and said, "Sit down!" Then she told me that MonaVie would be sending their private jet to pick us up, so that Lily would not have to fly on a commercial jet with all the germs. I couldn't believe it! I was screaming, Lily was screaming, and Joey was in happy shock. What a blessing!

The next day I got a call from the MonaVie pilot about scheduling the trip. I asked him what time the plane was leaving, and he laughed before answering, "Well, that's up to you!"

We scheduled the flight for that Friday at 10:00 a.m., and we were able to bring Lily's friend Hannah and our family friend Wendy. We were surprised again when the jet landed and pulled right up to the door of the airport to pick us up. I felt like the mom of a movie star as we boarded and chose comfortable seats in the plush, spacious cabin for the short flight to Orlando.

*Lily and her friend Hannah getting ready to board the MonaVie jet to Orlando, November 2009.*

The sun was shining and the day was perfect. Kelly Lyons, my new special friend, was there to pick us up and took us to the hotel. We got to the room, changed into shorts, and headed to the pool for lunch. We rested a bit after lunch and then got ready to venture out to Downtown Disney for some more fun. Lily tired quickly, so we returned to the hotel after dinner.

The next day we visited Sea World, and Sunday was the big fashion show. The show was sponsored by Kids Beating Cancer, and all the models were dressed like American Girl doll characters. Lily had a chance to get up on stage, tell her story, and pick the raffle tickets for all the prizes. She was beautiful!

Sadly, the day ended at 5:00 p.m. and it was time for us to go home. The consolation was that we got to ride in the fabulous MonaVie jet again, and we were home again by 6:00!

## Baptized!

This was November 2009, and Lily was in her fourth round of chemo. All this time, Lily kept the port on her chest, and my primary mission each day was to keep Lily away from germs and the dressing around the port clean.

One day, Lily came to me and asked if she could be baptized. Tears sprang to my eyes as I thought about my little girl and the beautiful step she was taking in her faith. My heart was thrilled that she would want to, but I was desperately worried about her port. However, I knew that if this was something she wanted to do, Joey and I would figure out a way to make it work.

First, I talked with our pastor, Steven Gibbs. I told him I wanted Lily baptized just like everyone else, fully dunked and immersed in the baptismal water. If we were going to do this, we were going to do it all the way! Then I talked to the doctor about how to protect Lily's port and keep it dry.

Lily was baptized on November 29, 2009. That morning, I wrapped Lily's torso completely in plastic wrap over her bandages, and we all headed to church. There were about twenty-seven people getting baptized; Lily was first in line and I was second. I had been baptized as a small child, but Lily's desire had ignited my own to be baptized again. In the midst of all we were going through, it was both a statement of my personal faith and trust in God and a submission to the Lord's plan for our future.

Lily had so many friends and family cheering for her as she stepped down into the water. I, of course, was standing next in line just bawling. She was dressed in a black Stonecreek Church t-shirt and a lime green bandana specially embroidered with a cross for the day. As she sat down in the water, Pastor Steven reached into his pocket and took out a matching bandana!

He put his own bandana on and then ever so gently, Pastor Steven tipped Lily's body back and submerged her for a moment in the water. Lily came up a moment later with a huge smile on her face. As I looked at her through my tears, I felt a peace come over me. In that moment, I knew that Lily belonged to God and that somehow, it would all be okay.

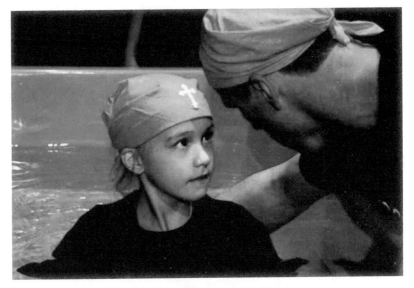

*Lily being baptized at Stonecreek Church.*

## All I Want for Christmas...

In December 2009, we were simultaneously planning for Christmas *and* for the surgery to remove what was left of Lily's tumor. The chemo treatments over the previous months had been steadily shrinking the main tumor, as well as the spots on her lung, bones, and bone marrow. Now, on December 21, we were waiting for the result of one more CT scan to tell us what size the tumor was.

That day, we went to TGI Fridays for lunch (because all Lily wanted to eat were the green beans at TGI Fridays). We were just getting our drinks when my phone rang, and it was the radiologist. He was so thrilled to tell me that the tumor had shrunk again—by two thirds! I was immediately in tears and could not control my emotions.

This was the greatest Christmas present I could ever receive!

While we were eating our lunch, I noticed Lily looking at the ceiling of the restaurant (if you've ever been in TGI Fridays, then you know the walls and ceiling are filled with stuff). I was asking Lily questions about how her food was and how she felt, and she just kept looking up at something. Finally, I asked her, "Lily, why do you keep looking up at the ceiling?"

She looked at me with that same Lily sparkle in her eye and said, "I am thanking God!"

There I was asking Lily about green beans, and she was praying and thanking God.... Of course, I apologized immediately for interrupting their conversation!

After that awesome news, we were able to take a deep breath and enjoy the holidays. On the 23rd, we went to the hospital to meet with Lily's surgeon to discuss removing the tumor. We were so blessed to work with Dr. Glasson; I really think she is the best surgeon on the planet. She is so caring—when she talked to Lily about what would happen in the operating room, it was obvious how much she cared. Then she let us know the surgery was scheduled for January 6th—just two weeks away.

7

# No Doodle Jump During Surgery

With Lily's surgery scheduled for right after the holidays, I can tell you the Andersons made very sure to have the merriest Christmas ever in 2009! On Christmas Eve, we were able to go to church together as a family, a privilege we once took for granted. We also visited Joey's parents at their house for a wonderful Christmas celebration after church. We couldn't stay too long at their house, but this time it had nothing to do with Lily's health. Santa was on his way, and our two girls were anxious to get home and get to bed!

The most beautiful Christmas present I could have imagined was watching Lily and Audrey run down the stairs on Christmas morning to see all the goodies Santa had left for them. Audrey had asked for a little play kitchen and there it was...pink, of course! Lily had asked Santa for a laptop; sure enough, he left one right by the fireplace. (Santa also left a bit of a mess...the girls were thrilled to see mysterious boot prints all around the fireplace hearth!)

Joey and I reveled in the girls' squeals of delight over the footprints and their exclamations over each present. The best sound was the mix of Audrey's little voice blending with Lily's big-sister tone as they played and laughed together. We all knew that a long road lay before us, and that Christmas morning was a wonderful, very thankful day.

January 6th came before we blinked...the day Dr. Glasson would do her best to remove whatever was left of Lily's tumor. We knew from the scans that the tumor had wrapped all around Lily's kidney; Dr. Glasson would try to save the kidney if she could. We also knew the surgery would be a long one. It was scheduled for 7:45 a.m., and would go for at least four hours.

Lily approached the day with her trademark style. She never shed a tear, and asked a ton of questions. When it was time to go into surgery, she gave Joey and me a thumbs-up. I hugged her as tightly as I could with all the wires and IV lines. Then Joey hugged her, and she asked him to do the Anderson Power Cheer. "How strong? Too strong!" They finished together, "Anderson Power!"

Before surgery, Lily also wrote a secret note to Dr. Glasson, and I helped her tape it to her stomach beneath the hospital gown. On lime green paper in Lily's confident handwriting, the note listed some specific instructions for surgery:

*Dear Dr. Glasson,*

*Just a few requests…*

*Please no tegaderm tape! It makes me itch.*

*Please take pictures of my tumor with your iPhone for my mommy and daddy.*

*Please play cool music while I am asleep. It helps make good dreams.*

*Please no Doodle Jump playing on the iPhone.*

*Steady hands, please!*

> *P.S. Love you!*
>
> OXOX
>
> *Lily*

Dr. Glasson told me later about discovering the note. She went in to the surgery room to join her team, all serious and scrubbed up. When they lifted Lily's gown and saw that bright lime green square in the middle of her tummy, several people exclaimed, "What is *that?!*" The nurse held it up for Dr. Glasson to read, and she just melted. (We have stayed in touch with Dr. Glasson, and she has that note from Lily on her refrigerator to this day.)

## A Look at the Monster

What was scheduled as a four-hour surgery ended up being almost nine hours long, in great part because of Dr. Glasson's great care and work to try and save Lily's kidney. In the end, though, the tumor was so wrapped up around the organ and so "sticky," Dr. Glasson thought it was safer to remove the kidney and make sure the entire tumor was gone.

Time stopped for just a moment when we saw Dr. Glasson finally coming out of surgery. I stared at her face, trying to read the outcome. Thankfully, she didn't leave us in suspense for long. I could see she was tired but smiling, and she simply said, "We got it all."

Did you notice one of Lily's instructions on the note? "Please take a picture of the tumor for my mom and dad." That may sound morbid, but I wanted to see it. I wanted to see this monster that was in Lily's body, this monster that we had been fighting so hard against. I still have the picture; it shows the tumor wrapped around the kidney and the tumor measures the length of a ruler, about twelve inches. Even then it was huge, after five months of chemo treatments to shrink it down. It was disgusting, and I felt so angry just looking at that evil thing. Angry but triumphant, because "we got it all"!

Lily was amazing when she woke up—so excited to see us, so strong. She was really happy to hear that Dr. Glasson got all of the tumor, and she was *so* hungry! I loved hearing that.

It was great to see Audrey loving on her sister and giving her a big kiss! It wasn't very easy to explain things to little Audrey. She knew what the hospital was—the big building with all the rooms. She got to come with us as often as we could take her, but there are strict rules about kids and ages on the oncology floor of the hospital. So...we snuck her in a lot! I know, I know, it's terrible! Little kids are germ factories! Maybe we shouldn't have done it, but Audrey was like our inspiration, our comic relief, and a bright spot of joy when all of us "adults"—I'm sure Lily thought of herself like that!—were weighted down with heavy "hospital" stuff. Lily loved it when Audrey got to come! So we'd sneak her as fast as we could into our room so that no one else would be exposed...and the nurses seemed to understand. They'd turn a blind eye and didn't give us trouble over it—we had enough trouble on our hands already.

Lily recovered from surgery very quickly. We were in a room in ICU for one night, and then they moved us to a regular room. She did so well, they sent us home after just three days. After all those months of fever, and blood transfusions, and midnight trips to the ER...to go home after this major surgery so quickly felt like one of the biggest miracles of all.


## It Will!

Removing the tumor was a major milestone. We had two more milestones to hit quickly after that: Lily's sixth and final chemo treatment, and the transplant of her own healthy stem cells back into her bone marrow to make new cancer-free blood.

She had done five chemo sessions, on five twenty-one day cycles. The treatments had greatly reduced the size of the tumor, the spots on her bones, and the cancer in her bone marrow. In order to do the stem cell transplant, though, her bone marrow had to be entirely clean of any cancer cells or else those healthy stem cells might mutate into cancer as well.

When Lily's cancer was first diagnosed, the cancer in her bone marrow was at 99 percent, meaning that for every ten bone marrow cells, nine of them were cancerous. We had watched those numbers shrink after each chemo treatment; now we were anxious to hear what remained for the final chemo treatment.

# glitter

I will never forget standing in the hallway of the hospital—we were there for our chemo, and Dr. George came out to me. He said, "Hey, we just got her bone marrow tests back." A few days prior, they had put Lily to sleep, put a long needle into her hip bones to extract the bone marrow, and tested it for cancer cells. Dr. George said, "There's still about 25 percent in her bone marrow."

We started at 99 percent, and were down to 25 percent. Down to 25 percent after five chemo treatments, with only one remaining to kill the rest of the cancer.

I asked him, "Is this one round of chemo going to get the 25 percent? That's all we have left."

With a doctor's honesty and bland directness, he replied, "Probably not."

I leaned into the Dr. George's face, looked into his eyes, and said, "*It will.*" Then I walked away.

That week Lily had her chemo. Afterward, we waited for the results of the all-important bone scan. In the meantime, we scheduled Lily's transplant and made plans to travel to Memphis for the eight-week stay at St. Jude's Hospital. Then it was just a waiting game for the bone test results.

That week, I got an e-mail from my sister, forwarded from a friend of a friend. A woman named Jenny, whom I have never met, wrote it. Jenny wrote that she had been following Lily's progress on our Care Pages, and was praying for Lily's recovery. She said she had run in "Lily's Run" back in October, and while she was running, the song "Everlasting God" had started playing on her iPod. As the song came on, she happened to be running on our street and saw Lily on the side of the road holding a big sign that said, "Thank you!" Jenny felt that that moment had been perfect timing, and prayed for Lily every time she heard that song on the radio. It was such a kind note, from someone I didn't even know, and it was such an encouragement.

I needed the encouragement. I was worn out physically and emotionally, and didn't even have the energy to get ready to go to church that Sunday. I lie in bed thinking of all the reasons I had not to go, and all the important ones that told me I should go…and then I got up to quickly get dressed. (Getting dressed quickly is no problem for me; I'm not much for fashion. Lily, with all her style and care over her clothes, would often look me up and down and ask, "Are you wearing…that?")

A few minutes before I planned to leave that Sunday, Lily came in and said she wanted to go to church, too! I hesitated, thinking of all the germs, but then decided that we both needed to be there. So off we went, and found our regular seats just a minute or two before the service started.

The first song began to play, and I fell back into my seat. It was "Everlasting God"! I started to cry and hugged Lily, so thankful for this little reminder that God was watching over us. Then Pastor Steven got up to preach; his message was "Purpose." He said that we each had a purpose here on earth, and it is our job to figure out what it is. He said the best way to determine our purpose is to think about what really bothers us in the world, and then work to change it. He said we all have a purpose to fix this broken world. It was part of living what Pastor Steven later called the "Yes Life." Lily squeezed my hand, and I squeezed back. We both knew our purpose was to *win* – to win against cancer, and to win against the darkness and fear that cancer brings with it.

## Zero

On February 10th, we were packed and ready to go to St. Jude when we got the call from the hospital. We were sitting in the parking lot at Costco when my phone rang. One of the nurse practitioners, Pam, said, "We got Lily's results back, and it was zero. You're going to Memphis!" Yes! I'll tell you now, if you were anywhere in the Southeastern United States and heard mysterious shouting on February 10th, that was the Andersons cheering and screaming at the top of their lungs!

We had made our plans for the transplant: My mom would travel with Lily and me and stay at St. Jude for the eight weeks we were to be there. Joey would stay home with Audrey and come up on the weekends to visit. Joey would continue with his cabinetry business. At this point, of course, I had stopped working in real estate and MonaVie; my full-time job was taking care of Lily. Changing bandages, administering pills and medications throughout the day according to schedule, cleaning ports and flushing lines…I had learned a lot about something I never wanted to know!

That's another thing about cancer. Not only does it invade your body and try to take over, it also invades your life and your family in every way imaginable. Your world becomes focused around this thing trying to take your life, and fighting it becomes as all-consuming as the cancer tries to be. Your conversation moves from school events and weekend plans to cell counts, hemoglobin, and words ending in "oma." I felt very overwhelmed, almost crushed by all of it, until I realized something: I may not have been taught to care for a cancer patient, but I was taught to love. I *could* love Lily with all my heart, and I didn't *need* to understand all the rest of it. The doctor's job was to treat the cancer, and my job was to take care of my girl. I *knew* how to do that.

Looking back, I am so very thankful that Joey's work allowed us to become a single-income family and supported us during that time. I will also be forever grateful for all the neighbors and friends who brought us delicious meals; there were days and weeks that I entirely forgot about cooking and eating for myself as I concentrated on Lily's chemo-induced nausea and the few things she could manage to keep down. (Besides that, if you know me, you know I'm not much of a cook. I can tell you that Joey and Audrey were even more grateful than I for all that wonderful food!)

## Transplant

On February 15th, 2010, we checked into St. Jude. Lily was ready and determined for the stem cell transplant. She had beaten the tumor in her abdomen and the cancer in her bone marrow. She had just a couple of spots left on her bones, and we could see on the bone scans that they were also closing up. She could see the finish line, and was eager to do the transplant and get back to her regular life.

We didn't know at that point how hard the next four weeks were going to be. When you go to have a stem cell transplant, you are first given a chemo session that brings your body down to absolute zero. Your immune system is basically dead; you can't get better. Then they infuse your stem cells back into your body, and it looks like a bag of blood. The stem cells are injected through a syringe right into the chest port and they go right into the blood on the way to the bone marrow. I just envision those stem cells going in like an invading army, shouting, "Come on! It's time to make healthy blood!"

Before the transplant, though, Lily had to endure that horrible chemo. She had sores in her mouth, down her throat, diarrhea, tubes hooked up to her everywhere. She was so weak she couldn't walk, and her skin was burning from all the chemicals inside her. It literally looked like she had sunburn all over her body.

To help soothe the burns, we gave her a daily sitz bath. One day, as Mom and I were getting Lily to the bathroom for her bath, I noticed that Lily seemed especially weak. We slowly made our way to the tub, and just as I said, "Here, Lily, sit down," she suddenly turned blue-grey and collapsed. For one second, I thought we had lost her. Like some sort of Olympian, I leaped over the hospital bed and ran out in the hallway in total panic, screaming, "She's dying! What's happening? She's dying!"

Nurses came within seconds, got Lily back into bed, and started IV lines dripping (we found out later that her little body was simply exhausted and dehydrated). In just a few minutes, Lily came blinking slowly back to consciousness, and I gave her a big smile of encouragement and relief. In my heart, though, that moment made me realize that no matter how positive we were, no matter how hard we fought, there was a chance that Lily could die.

Over the next weeks before the transplant, Lily was so, so sick. She was bedridden, too weak to move. We just watched the IV lines drip and prayed for the day Lily could have her transplant. Those weeks were hell. Hell for Lily, as her body was ravaged and burned by the chemo. Hell for me, as I helplessly watched my baby lie so close to death. And hell for Joey as he got up each day, took care of Audrey, went to work after the nanny got to our house, and tried to carry on with "normal life" single-handedly. His family was separated, and he had to keep it all together.

Joey and Audrey came to visit each weekend, but had to look at Lily through a glass window. Lily was like the boy in the plastic bubble with no immune system; the doctors couldn't allow a single germ to come close to her—so no sneaking Audrey in this time. They did allow Audrey in to visit one time, though, right before Lily's transplant. The nurses wrapped three-year-old Audrey in a big hospital gown from head to toe and covered her face with a surgical mask. All you could see was her blue eyes. They let Lily hug her briefly, and then took Audrey quickly back to the waiting room.

March 1 was the day of the transplant. After the drama of the last few weeks, I was surprised at how simple and quick the actual procedure was. At 10:30 a.m., the nurses administered some Benadryl in case Lily had a skin reaction to the preservative in the stem cells. A few minutes later, more nurses came in with a small freezer containing Lily's stem cells and a little warmer to thaw them. At 10:59 a.m., the doctor came in to check and recheck the cells with the info on Lily's armband. Then at 11:00 a.m. sharp, the nurse asked Lily, "Are you ready?" Lily responded, "Yes!" and they immediately injected the stem cells through a syringe right into Lily's line. It took all of four minutes to complete!

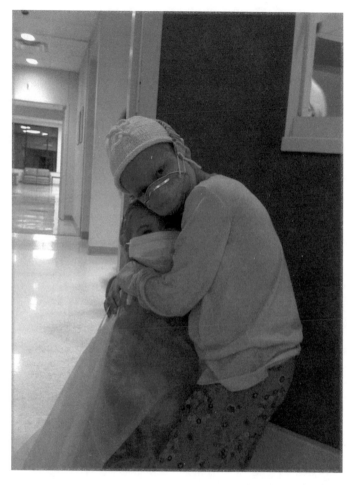

*Lily and Audrey hugging at St. Jude Hospital after not seeing each other for so long.*

## Places to Be, Things to Do

When we went in on February 14th, Lily told them that she had a fashion show to be in on March 31st—she was *determined* to get through it and make that fashion show. "I have to be home by the end of March because I'm in a fashion show for the Rally Foundation," she told them, "and there's football players from the Falcons going to walk me down an aisle and so I got to be home."

They told me that she probably was not going to be able to make it home for the show. But they didn't know Lily.

Lily's hemoglobin levels, having been reduced to nothing, had to rebound to a certain level in order for them to release her. Remember, her entire immune system was intentionally brought down, putting her at risk to germs, so her white blood cells had to recover before she could be released.

We were getting close to the end of March, and she wasn't quite there. I could tell how badly she wanted it, and she did everything in her power to get better. She was so close....

Then, just days before the show, the doctor came to me and said, "We know you want to go home—just be careful. Don't overdo it." And they let us go home!

We had places to be and things to do. Lily was incredibly excited to make a very special trip that would put her on stage in front of hundreds of the best entrepreneurs in the world. Was she worried or anxious? Not a bit!

8

# "YES" As a Family

It was never in Lily to stay down or to make it about herself. She was too busy living!

In April, we had a garage sale in our neighborhood, and Lily set up a lemonade stand under a sign that said, "All proceeds will go to the MORE Project." It was her idea, and she made the poster.

*Lily with her lemonade stand for the MORE Project.*

Our family heard about the MORE Project through MonaVie, and it has helped to change the lives of tens of thousands of people by providing some of Brazil's most impoverished families with food, shelter, clothing, and education. I tried to paint a picture for Lily of what life was like for these kids—that they didn't have American Girl dolls, perhaps toys at all, and often not even shoes. She had fifteen pairs of sandals.

And Lily just *got it*. She understood what it meant that those kids didn't even have shoes, so even though *she* had cancer, she wanted to help them.

Lily raised $121, of which she didn't even ask to keep a penny, 50 cents per cup of lemonade. Except people were tossing in twenties. They would ask, "What's the MORE Project?" and she would just tell them about the kids in Brazil who don't have anything. People who didn't even want lemonade donated!

And that brought us to a darkened auditorium with over 3,000 people in it. Every eye was on our precious Lily, with her bald, bandana-covered head, agonizingly slim features…and incredible confidence and strength of purpose. She made her way confidently across the stage. Just nine years old, with delicate features and stylish bandana covering the baldness from her chemotherapy treatments, she didn't fit the usual mold of a business convention speaker. Her confidence and strength of purpose, however, were the equal of any driven and successful entrepreneur in the room. Her audience sat in rapt attention as she stood in the spotlight and took the microphone with a huge smile.

"Hi! I'm Lily Anderson! I raised $121 for the MORE Project with a lemonade stand."

Debbie Kalb, a significant leader in MonaVie and host of the conference, stood next to Lily on stage. Debbie took the microphone next.

"Guys, this is Lily. She's fighting cancer and still raised $121 to help provide shelter, food, and clothing for homeless children in Brazil. So, what can we do?"

The audience stirred, and person after person began taking out checkbooks to write their own donation of $121. Enthusiasm and excitement swept through the auditorium, and the little girl stood grinning on stage and watching delightedly.

At the end of that evening, she'd helped raise $35,000 for charity.

That was in April 2010. The conference was the annual MonaVie Elevate Conference, and the little girl…well, that's my Lily.

Lily's enthusiasm for helping the children in Brazil was infectious, and told a room of entrepreneurs how she, a little girl fighting cancer, had determined to make a difference. The people just responded to her. It was incredible. People lifted us up emotionally. Rex Crain—this incredible guy—prayed with her, and the entire experience was amazing.

It just showed me so clearly what it's like when we choose to help others—no matter what we're going through. Lily had so much against her, so many reasons she could have felt sorry for herself or just isolated from the world around her. Instead, she chose to embrace those whose need was greater than her own and help *others* to live a "YES!" life!

## Hold Your Breath

The round of chemo at St. Jude, which had brought her down to zero, had likely killed even more cancer; we were done. For now. The only thing she had left to do was a treatment called antibody therapy, which we did at Egleston Children's Hospital back in Atlanta. Dr. Katzenstein headed up this stage, and he explained that this antibody or hormone was derived from rats, and it was shown to prevent neuroblastoma.

Lily's reaction? "Am I going to grow whiskers like a rat?" She'd already had a hard time with antibody therapy—it is a five-cycle treatment and is very painful to your nerves. She had to do it in the hospital, and it was very hard on her remaining kidney—nearly shutting it down—and only made it through four cycles.

We had done a year-and-a-half in a year. Lily, whom they said had six months to live, had outlived their expectations and had been through hell. It was the end of October, and Lily had come through everything they threw at her—with a smile. We were so proud of her.

We'd have scans every three months, but for now, she was done. When I looked at her, I had a hard time holding back the tears—so thin, so sick after all the harsh treatments. But we'd made it.

Hadn't we?

## Oh No, Not Again...

We were to have scans every three months to keep a very close eye on Lily's recovery. We'd been through so much, but we had to remain ever vigilant.

And on our very first scan, they saw something tiny on her pelvis. "We're not sure what it is," they told me. "It could be some scar tissue showing up, we're not sure. Let's do another scan in February." Can you hold your breath for three months? I felt like I tried.

February came, and we were back in for another scan.

The spot was bigger. The cancer was back, on the bone of her pelvis. We would have to start over again.

Lily was nine, and her hair had just started to grow back in—she had a short little curly bob. She was healthy, running around, back in school. After missing all of third grade because of this nightmare, she was in fourth grade with everything starting to return to normal. She'd had surgery to get the port out, but as March rolled around, we learned we would be headed back in for another surgery to put a port in.

Lily had to go back to the radiation clinic to get "marked" for her treatment, and the doctor told us all the side effects of radiation. I really didn't want to know all the things he told us, but I'm sure it is required. I couldn't help but watch Lily as the doctor told us all this, my heart was aching for her.

She was mad, sad, scared, and confused—all at the same time. I just felt like crying for her, but Joey said it perfectly, as usual: "If we are strong, Lily is strong. If we fall apart, Lily will fall apart."

While Lily is awash in a lot of different emotions, one had surfaced to the top for me: I was *mad*. Not at the doctors, Joey, or certainly Lily—I was furious with cancer and all the crap that was happening to my baby because of it. Someone gave me some really good advice, however, and I ran with it: *Use it.* Channel that energy to help me fight this with Lily.

Lily tackled getting a new port like she did so many other things—like a champ! She is my hero, over and over. She was nervous when we arrived, but Joey talked her through it. The best part about her surgery was that she knew Dr. Glasson was the surgeon, and that put her at ease. Dr. Julie Glasson is the amazing doctor who performed Lily's first biopsy and took out her horrible tumor back in January of last year. She is one fantastic person!

Dr. Glasson came into the room for a little pre-op meeting, and Lily's face lit up! It was so funny to hear Lily talk to her like Julie was her big sister. They talked about iPhones and Hello Kitty things first. Lily then instructed her where to put the port—and *not* to put any tape on it because she would get a rash! Joey and I could have left the room and let them hash it out by themselves! I was so proud of Lily. She then asked questions about how it would feel and if it can move under her skin. Lily was very serious about the placement, though. She wanted it where *no one* could see it, even when wearing a bikini! Hilarious!

She came through with flying colors and woke up *starving!* I love it when she eats...and it stays down.

## Seventy-two Hours of Bliss

We had a fantastic weekend in Nashville celebrating Uncle Shane and Autumn's wedding! It was so great to be in the presence of family after going through such a rough week at home! All the girls went together to get pretty at the hair salon, which was right up Lily's alley, laughing and giggling all day—until it was *show time!*

As family, we got to the church early to get pictures and front row seats, but when the guests started coming in, I saw a beautiful woman in the back, sitting next to Uncle Tom. It took me a second to recognize that it was Barbara Mandrell!

Even though Lily and I watched Autumn get ready, when she came out, we both gasped: she was just stunning! My brother was going to die when he saw her! My Lily was very beautiful, too, as she got up and read a poem.

I had the chance to talk to Barbara, which was incredible— including the questionable confession that my sisters and I had played Barbara Mandrell and the Mandrell Sisters! When I told her I always had to be Louise, because I had darker hair, she laughed and said that was the best anyway since she was still active.

She complemented me on Lily's poem and her adorable hair. I told her that she just got her hair back because she was fighting cancer. Barbara was so sweet—she grabbed my hand and said a prayer for Lily right there!

We danced the night away, and I watched Lily the whole night with a smile from ear to ear. She got to meet so many fun people and danced with everyone who was on the dance floor! It truly was seventy-two hours of bliss. Sunday was hard; we had to head home, and tears flowed freely.

It had been an ideal break, but we had to start our battle with our monster Monday morning.

## Could We Say "YES" At Home?

Through all this, Joey and I faced a different set of questions about what *we* would choose. In a way, I feel like it really wasn't a choice at all.

We actually faced some steep odds of our own.

There was nothing wrong with our marriage when Lily got sick. But people can often think their marriage is fine...until their kid gets cancer. Remember that I didn't want to know the odds when the doctor was telling us about Lily's chances? Well, I didn't want to know them about marriages surviving having a child with cancer, either.

But I found out. Three in four of them fail. They fall apart. Lily faced her odds, but Joey and I were facing ours, as well. When it came down to it, how could we face a fight for the life of our marriage any differently than our child was facing a life-threatening illness?

We chose "YES" in our marriage.

While cancer or other major illnesses can splinter a family, for us, it drew us together. Instead of pushing us apart, it pulled us closer.

The hospitals know the odds, too, and we had social workers asking us all the time, "How's your marriage?" or "Is there any violence in the home?" Chaplains even try to get information, and they all mean well—but at times it felt like the Inquisition!

You want to say, "We're good, we've got to deal with this," and just dismiss their concerns—except that their concerns are valid. I don't want to understate how profoundly having a child who is so sick with cancer—how spending days and weeks apart, how having to focus your energy completely and totally on one person—can impact your relationship.

Joey and I got married in 2000, and we'd both been busy living our lives when this happened. He had his business, I was in real estate and MonaVie—we had full lives. We loved our kids, had just had another precious little girl, and were living the cliché American dream.

But when Lily got sick, I remember just locking eyes with Joey and saying, "We've got to keep this together." They'd told us how many marriages fall apart, but we knew we had to choose "YES" just as much as Lily was.

We've had our ups and downs, just like anyone else. But when I say we had to make a choice, I think I don't do it justice: Just like quitting on Lily was never an option, we were in this together—failure was not an option. Ever.

We weathered the ups and downs, the highs and lows. There were times I thought that I was going to kill him...and I'm sure he felt the same way toward me. But we knew that we couldn't attack each other at a time like this for something stupid like not taking out the trash or being late. We tackled the treatments together; the home life together; the travel and hospitals and all the killer little pitfalls that can start small but become large *together*. No one fought the battle with cancer alone in our family; we all fought side by side by side—against cancer, not against each other.

Too many people let the divide start with little things—things that aren't even worth it. And when your child's life is on the line, when your marriage's life is on the line, there is absolutely no room for fighting over dumb, little things.

Nor is there room for the alternative. If you want to survive, there is one choice and only one: You've got to choose "YES"!

I know we are blessed to have a different ending to the story of our marriage. We've been to enough funerals; we were determined this disease would not claim any part of our family.

It would not take our marriage.

Lily would often tell us, "Things happen for a reason," and in the middle of our nightmare, our relationship grew closer—but so did our relationship with God. Our faith grew *stronger* as we fought this enemy, death.

Lily died thinking this—*things happen for a reason*. And I'm perfectly okay with that.

So I guess I want to know why this all happened to us. I can't wait to get to heaven and find out, but there is a reason that Joey and Audrey and I are now here and she is in heaven shining down on us. There's some reason.

The thing is, life is short. You don't have time to sit around wondering why. You just have time to *live*, because you never know when your last day will be. You don't have time to waste asking "why."

You just have time to say "YES" to life.

# 9

# Life in Pencil

In early April we headed back to the hospital for Lily's first week of chemo and radiation combination—as though one alone isn't hard enough to handle! What we didn't know was that the nurses typically access the port for the child on the first day of the chemo round and leave the needle in the port until the final day. In Lily's case it meant accessing the port on Monday and deaccessing it on Friday after her last infusion.

The port she had was under her skin, so when we went to the clinic, we put numbing cream on her skin so she won't feel the needle going in. The needle was connected to a tube that the nurses can of course use to infuse medicine, but they can also draw blood from it when her counts need to be checked. It was quite handy.

Because it was under the skin when it was not in use, Lily could do almost anything—no bungee jumping or other crazy stunts!—but she could swim, so that would make this summer a bit nicer. Well, when Lily heard that the nurses were planning to leave the access needle in until Friday to make things easier, she flipped! I mean *flipped!*

You see, my little hero was a lot smarter this time around and absolutely would *not* let them leave the needle accessed for the whole week. She told them that they would have to take it out each night before she went home. They told her they don't do that, and she said, "Well, you are going to do it this time! I am not leaving this hospital with this accessed!" They wanted to leave it because of the risk of infection, and every time they put the needle in, it could get infected. But she didn't care!

At first I tried to explain to Lily that we need to follow the policy of the hospital, but she did not care. I realized that Lily rarely got to make decisions through this whole thing, and if she got to make one decision to have some control over her world, I wanted to let her do it.

It was coming *out!*

The nurses all were *so* gracious, and one of Lily's favorites, Sarah, came in and she told Lily that she understood how hard it was not being able to make any decisions, so the staff had decided to let Lily make the decision about her port! They did check with me first, but if it was going to make her go home in peace, it was worth the extra time and effort. Sometimes we just need to let the kiddos feel important, too. *Impressive!*

Needless to say, the port came out every night and was put back in every day when we got there. The weeks of treatments went about as well as could be expected, but I'm afraid Lily is allergic to the smell of "hospital"—just smelling it now makes her want to throw up. Can't say that I blame her!

From the time we pulled up to the parking deck, she would feel sick. She would hold her iPhone in one hand and use the other to hold her nose—all the way to the clinic room! The nurses and doctors knew that she needed a room where they could close the door, not just a curtain partition, and try to shut out the smell of "hospital."

Her famous line in the hospital was, "Close the door! Close the door!" Doctors and nurses would try to slip through a crack in the door as quickly as they could because she just couldn't handle the smell of all the medicine, blood, "hospital," and the fast food people had brought in all mixing together.

## Food for the Soul

We tried to enjoy our spring break, but we had lots of doctors appointments. We just took it a day at a time and tried to make each day fun. We saw the movie "Soul Surfer," which we all enjoyed. But while most kids walked out saying, "I am *never* going surfing because I might get bitten by a shark!" Lily had a really different reaction.

She had tears in her eyes, and when I asked her what was wrong, she told me, "Mommy, that movie made me realize how important it is that I don't give up!" So then I was crying, too, and so was Nana, who was with us to visit. I was so amazed by Lily every day. Of all the things she could have said...

## Birthday Plans in Pencil

Whoever it was that said "Life should be written in pencil" was *right!*

Early one morning, as I was helping Lily fix her hair, I noticed a lot of strands on my hands. I tried to pretend it was nothing, but Lily saw it on my face.

Her hair was starting to fall out again.

This was devastating to my brave girl. You see, Lily had been planning her tenth birthday for about six months and had talked about this party every single day! We were planning for Memorial Day weekend, right after school got out. Lily wanted a "BLACK AND WHITE PARTY WITH A RED CARPET FASHION SHOW" (in all capital letters, naturally). All the girls would get their hair and makeup done and then strut down the red carpet in their dresses. The cake was planned, the music, the dresses, the food, the photographer—everything!

Her hair falling out ruined those wonderful plans, and suddenly I felt so ANGRY. Angry that Lily would lose her hair again…that I couldn't fix it for her…that all of our plans forevermore had to made in pencil.

I fell apart when I got home from dropping Lily off at school—and decided that the party *would* happen. It would just have to be *before* her hair was gone. We would have it that Saturday…less than four days away!

I immediately got on the phone with some of her closest friends' moms and explained the last-minute birthday party plans. When I picked Lily up that day at noon for chemo treatment, I told her about the change in plans. The smile on her face lit up the car! We made plans together the whole way to the hospital. We explained to the nurses and asked for their input as well.

By the end of her chemo treatment the cake was ordered, the photographer booked, a friend scheduled to do hair and makeup for the girls, and even some special surprise guests (Lily didn't know that Uncle Shane, Aunt Autumn, and my parents were driving hours to come to the party as well).

## "Style" Anderson

Saturday morning I woke up feeling like the mother of the bride! My sister, Kristin, arrived with the biggest tank of helium I had ever seen—and two *hundred* balloons. Have you ever imagined two hundred floating balloons filling your house? I can tell you, it was a sight to behold. Kristin covered the ceiling with black and white balloons and made a huge balloon arch outside for the girls to walk under.

Lily's outfit, of course, was fabulous. She wore a dress some very special friends had given her—identical triplets who had matching dresses they'd worn to their thirteenth birthday party. Lily had seen it at the Spratlin triplets' party, and they gave her one of the matching, beautiful dresses. I thought I could get away with a pair of jeans, but "Style" Anderson knew better than that. She quickly had me put together impeccably in a black sundress and red high heels, and Joey in a black t-shirt and jeans (he was afraid she would make him get a tux!)

Seventeen giggly girls soon arrived, and were quickly settled in Hair and Makeup. Then we headed outside for some dancing and the Red Carpet Fashion Show! Each girl walked down the carpet and did a signature move while Shane described all of their outfits. Hats, sparkles, feather boas, oversized glasses—

never has New York City's Fashion Week seen such a display! And *never* has a red carpet been filled with so much joyful, laughing ten-year-old fun.

Lily went to bed that night tired—but so happy. It was an amazing birthday, regardless of the day on the calendar. It didn't matter when we made the memories, as long as we made them together.

*Lily's tenth birthday party.*

## Take Nothing for Granted

Lily's precious tiny curls started coming out soon after. Oh, how I hated to see them go! We cried together and then decided to turn it into a positive. We decided that it just meant the chemo was working and shrinking the tumor!

I have to admit that having hair is something I took for granted. I think we all do until we are faced with this kind of situation. Never again will I complain about a bad hair day! Never again should you wish for curlier or straighter or longer hair. When a thought like that pops in your head, turn it immediately around and just say "thank you" for the hair God gave you!

Throughout this journey, I have heard from many people, "I don't know how you can do this!" or "How do you stay so strong?" or "I could never do what you are doing!" Well...I am here to tell you that ALL OF YOU would do it if you had to!

There really is no choice. We were dealt these cards, and we will play the hand until we win! There is no quitting, there is no giving up. There is no complaining about the cards. You just keep going! After all, what is the alternative?

It is not easy. Some days feel mired in quicksand, and everything is slow and sluggish. Some days I feel so angry! Some days I cry...a lot. A parent with a sick baby has special tear ducts that are built to last longer, I feel certain. But crying only gets me down, and nowhere. So I wipe the tears and push forward. All the babies battling cancer right now are stronger than any grown-up could ever be, so who I am to complain?

We reached a point soon after Lily's birthday party when she had to make that choice for herself. Lily had done it all before; she knew what would happen and how it would feel. She hated the hospital, she hated needles, and she hated being sick!

As we arrived at the hospital for the next chemo treatment, Lily began to sob. "I don't want to do this!!" she said ferociously. I wrapped my arms around her, squeezed her, and told her it would be okay.

That only made her cry harder. "I don't want to go, Mom! Please! Please!!"

Before I thought about the words, they escaped my mouth. "Okay, Lily, if you don't want to do it today, then let's go home!"

The words came out so fast that it made my head spin. What did I just say to her? What on earth was I going to do if she went back to the car?

She stopped in her tracks, looked up at me with huge tears in her eyes and said, "Really?"

I took a deep breath. "Lily, if you want to quit, then quit. If you want to ruin your summer, stop the treatments. BUT…if you want to finish this and get it done, let's go to the clinic and do your treatment."

It was a very long three seconds of silence. My heart knew she would keep fighting, but I was a tiny bit scared she might turn around and get in the car. What would I do then?

After one more second, my brave girl took a breath and stepped towards the hospital, into another round of chemo. Anderson Power!!

Lily completed that round, and her third round a month later like a true champion. I'll tell you though… when she heard the beep-beep-beep of the infusion machine indicating we were done, Lily was up and darting out the door faster than I could say, "Disney, here we come!" And with that, we were off to Orlando for Lily's Make a Wish trip and her tenth birthday.

# 1 0

# A Chance to Be Normal

Once again, when we learned the cancer was back, our lives were changed—and I had no control. When Lily was diagnosed the first time, we were devastated. The second time you are told your child has cancer, you're devastated—and *angry*. I was just so angry because I couldn't do anything to fix my baby.

I felt guilty even taking five minutes to fix my hair when I knew she wouldn't have any shortly. I felt compelled to sleep with her every single night so I could hold her. I felt sad that Audrey didn't get all of me. I had no desire to do very much, because all I could do was try to figure out how to fix this. I was trying not to shut everyone out, but I was just completely overwhelmed by this disease. My heart was hurting constantly.

But while the darkness is so dark, the bright spots shine all the brighter.

## Disney

Lily finished her third round of chemo on May 13, and before our big trip to Disney, we had a few days on the beach near

Charleston for my nephews' birthdays to decompress. My mom rode back with us to Atlanta, and we all got ready for our Make a Wish trip to Disney World!

On Friday the 20th the entire Anderson gang, plus one Nana, jumped into a minivan and made the trek to Orlando. It was a very *long* ride, but the minivan made it a tiny bit easier to get up and help the kids with everything they needed. I mean, seriously, how many snacks can two children need in a seven-hour trip? We stopped in Lake City to drop Lily off with our friends, who were meeting us in Disney the next morning. Lily wanted to spend the night with them and finish her ride to Disney in their car, and I have to admit that heading to the hotel without her felt very strange to me.

Saturday morning, we met back up with Lily and the Kalb family at Universal—and proceeded to tackle every roller coaster in the park! I loved watching Lily—she did not stop the entire day! She rode the same ride six times in a row, and while all of us were wiped out, Lily was eager for more! I was so proud of her, and I loved seeing her energy.

The next day was Sea World! After spraying an entire bottle of sunscreen on Lily and Audrey, we were ready to take over the park. We saw all the shows, and once again Lily rode *every* roller coaster she could. She even got us all on the water rides! By that point we were all so *hot* that it didn't matter.

I did have one rule, though: No one was allowed to complain about being hot at Disney. It was, after all, Florida—warm weather is kind of the point! We'd been to Disney several times, and we always discussed along the way that no one was allowed to say, "I'm hot" at Disney. *Everybody's* hot at Disney!

After taking a day off just to rest—*ahhhhhh*—we were ready for the Magic Kingdom, where Audrey braved the heat dressed as Snow White and sporting a black wig *all day!* The following day was Animal Kingdom—Lily made me ride Mt. Everest, which is crazy, five times—and again, she didn't stop the entire day. Our final day, we were back at the Magic Kingdom to hit the best rides again and catch up to the princesses we didn't see the first day. Audrey was old enough to appreciate all the princesses and ride the rides, and it was so fun to watch her face light up when she got their autographs!

We celebrated Lily's actual tenth birthday while there in Orlando. I couldn't believe that it had been ten years ago when, at 4:04 a.m., our little hero entered the world! Lily had me wake her up at exactly 4:04 a.m. to wish her a happy birthday, but she didn't stay awake long.

I didn't go straight back to sleep, however. I just watched her for a time, soaking up the time together with her peaceful and asleep. Just a normal, sweet little sleeping child.

I wished those days wouldn't end. It wasn't just the fun of the parks and friends; it was that for a while, we were *normal.* We weren't a family battling a deadly disease, and Lily wasn't a kid locked in mortal combat with cancer. She was just a precious little girl, full of life and energy.

Real life, with all its challenges and demands, was waiting for us to return. I knew a mound of laundry would be calling my name. Even so, it was nice to get back to our familiar and comfortable home...

Until we found ourselves in the emergency room, Lily burning up with a fever of 103. She'd had a little cough the night before, but no fever; then, while at a BBQ with friends, she'd been so tired she could hardly pick her head up.

Reality had been paused, it seemed, while we were away, but strong antibiotics to cover an infection and a delayed round of chemo seemed to have been just waiting to pour down rain on our vacation buzz.

The fight had resumed.

# Joshua

We were hoping that a special test called the MIBG would show where Lily's cancer was and enable a different treatment in Ohio. We had tried it early on, and it hadn't worked then either; but I had held out a small hope that perhaps something in Lily's body had changed and *this time* it would work. The doctor thought it was worth a try.

The day we would find out if the MIBG scan worked, my body just woke up at 5:08 in the morning. I was sleeping with Lily…when I suddenly *sat up*. I felt something telling me to go grab my Bible. Now, I'm not an early-morning Bible reading kind of person, so this was kind of strange.

I always make coffee first thing in the morning because I'm just a coffee person, so I got started making the coffee. While I got the coffee ready, I was praying silently. I knew that we were going to get the answer about the test that day, so I was asking for help to get through the day.

Any time you're expecting a call from a doctor as the parent of a sick child, you're just a neurotic mess. The waiting game is actually worse than finding out the answer, so I was just praying for help.

I picked up my Bible, and there was a business card stuck in it. I don't ever put business cards in my Bible, so that was weird. I opened it to where the card was and looked at it. It was for Josh Robins, a guy who worked with my brother in Nashville. I had no idea why his business card would be in my Bible.

Then I looked under the card to where my Bible had opened up. It was the first page of the Book of Joshua. I was still sleepy, so I wasn't yet putting anything together, but I thought perhaps it was something from God so I started reading. I soon got to the ninth verse, which says, "This is my command—be strong and courageous! Do not be afraid or discouraged. For the Lord your God is with you wherever you go."[2]

This was my answer! The moment I read it, I was sure that we'd get good news about the MIBG test. I was all happy, because I felt like this was confirmation that things were going to go great.

Later that morning, I headed to the gym, but I couldn't be gone too long because a pastor named Roger Houtsma was going to come to our house later. My friends had begged me to have him talk with Lily to encourage her. I'd put it off for some time, but today was the day. I started thinking that maybe this pastor would pray over Lily and God would heal her.

So I headed to the gym, and I'd barely been there twenty minutes when my phone rang during my class. It was the doctor.

---

[2] Joshua 1:9.

The MIBG scan had not worked, and we would need to come up with a different plan. We wouldn't be going to Ohio.

I fell apart. *This wasn't how it was supposed to go!*

As I got home, I was as deflated as I had been encouraged earlier. I was crying and so discouraged. I almost called to cancel the pastor's visit, but I decided to take a shower first. And before I knew it, he was ringing my doorbell!

My girlfriends who had told me about him both came as well, so we were sitting with Pastor Roger as he talked to Lily about all the sick people he has prayed for and how he traveled around the world praying for people.

"Many people with cancer have been healed when I prayed for them," he told her.

I wanted to come out of my skin! I was tensing up inside, because he was telling this to a ten-year-old girl! These were strong words to tell a sick little girl desperate to be well, and I didn't want her getting completely discouraged if his words proved untrue for her.

So he started telling her about a little boy who had had leukemia. His name was Joshua…

*His name is Joshua?* I sat back in my chair, my eyes filling with tears. *Maybe this would be okay,* I thought.

"He had leukemia when he was little, and now he's twenty-seven," Pastor Roger told Lily. "God healed him. I didn't heal him; God did. There's hope, Lily."

When Lily heard what the boy's name was, she wanted me to tell Pastor Roger about my experience that morning. Lily believed so strongly in God! Sometimes I think she was a stronger believer than I am!

So I told him about it, and he nodded his head. "Those are called tokens from God," he told Lily. "God speaks to us, but He doesn't just tell us one time and then forget it—He'll say things three, four, five times. Those are tokens." He explained that was why I had been seeing Joshua all day and then again in his story— it was God telling us He was with us.

"My mommy told me those were called 'Whispers,'" Lily told him. She was confirming with the pastor, who knew more than Mommy.

"Yes, that's perfect!" he said. "'Whispers' is a great word for it." Then he asked, "Lily, can I put my hand on your forehead and pray over you?"

So he prayed this long, beautiful prayer. When I pray, the words do *not* come out sounding like this, but he has had lots of practice, and it flowed and was beautiful. When he was done, we were all crying.

Lily jumped up off the couch and ran into the bathroom. When she came back, she was absolutely dripping sweat. "Mommy, it's so hot in here!" she said. She was wiping her forehead, and she had circles of sweat under her armpits. Little girls do not soak their shirts with sweat for no reason! *What was going on?*

Roger was smiling as he said, "Sometimes when the Holy Spirit is present, people feel a sense of heat go through their bodies."

Now I was completely freaked out, wondering what was happening. Roger prayed again, and I thanked him for coming as he headed to the door. But before he left, he told Lily to watch for signs and changes in how she felt.

I do not think that Lily really understood how sick she was. How could she, at ten years old? She didn't let the sickness get her down, but she hated being bald. Remember, this is "Style" Anderson we're talking about here!

Well, two weeks after Pastor Roger's visit, to the day, Lily and I were in the powder room together. She was brushing her teeth, and as I watched, suddenly I noticed something. "Lily, come here!" I told her. I looked at her head closely.

There was *hair* growing on her head—little peach fuzz hairs I could see with the lights out and a flashlight. Lily was still on high dose chemotherapy. She shouldn't have any hair growing on her head at all. There was no reason for it!

Her hair was growing back in! From that time forward, her hair grew back in—curly brown hair, even with the high doses of chemo.

God hadn't healed Lily the way we hoped. However, the cancer stopped growing at that point and didn't come back for about a year.

We can see, looking back, that this little hair miracle was just a way of God showing us that He was with us. Whatever happened, whatever bad reports we got, we could take courage from the fact that our God is with us wherever we go.

## Return to Reality

So Lily scanned negative for the second time—which didn't mean that she had no cancer, just that she was one of the 2 percent of people who just show negative. We wouldn't be going to Ohio, and our treatment options were growing thin.

Without the option of the MIBG treatment, the doctors advised us to go back to what we had been doing. So we resumed the same drugs that she had the last few rounds because, even though her spots of cancer weren't gone, there were no new areas. I wasn't sure how I felt about this. Wouldn't we want to try something *new* if the old stuff wasn't beating the cancer? Why would we do the same thing if it didn't work?

When I asked the doctors about this, they came back with some chilling words. They told us how few options we had left to try. They told us that they didn't want to ever have to say the words, "There's nothing else we can do."

The crazy mom came out of me when they said this. "Please," I begged, "don't ever say those words to me again!"

The room went silent for a few moments that seemed like hours. I looked into each doctor's eyes to make sure each had heard me and then broke the silence with, "Okay?"

I tried to make light of the moment after that, but for a moment I'd realized that I was sitting in a conference room where many times parents have heard those very words about their own kids. *There's nothing more we can do.* I hated those words like profanity.

Thankfully, we had a very full life. Lily was living every moment to its fullest, and we were counting down to one of the biggest events in her life—singing from a national stage to tens of thousands of people. Live!

But first, we would be sung *to*.

## American Idol Miracle

We had received tickets to the American Idol concert in Atlanta, and we arrived early for a "meet and greet" with the performers before the show. The idols were at a table signing autographs, and we were rushed through the room so quickly we didn't really get a chance to take pictures or say hello to the performers.

Even so, we were bursting with excitement as we went to get our tickets from Will Call—until I saw the woman's face behind the counter when she couldn't find tickets under our name. I watched Lily's face go from the biggest smile *ever* to fighting back tears.

I was just about ready to max out my American Express card when a miracle happened. A man stepped in front of me and asked, "Do you guys need two tickets? We got six, but we're only going to need four of them." I'm pretty sure he came straight from heaven!

As we approached the seats, which were excellent, he explained to me that his kids were going to sit down on the floor and asked if Lily would like to join them. Should I let my sick little daughter sit with complete strangers?

I could see where they'd be sitting from our seats, so I agreed. Lily was so incredibly excited, and I was just overwhelmed—the tears started to come.

But wait, it gets better. Linda, with whom I'd talked in the lobby, told me she was a writer and would get to go up in the pit for most of the show. She offered to take my camera and get some pictures, then get it back to me after the show. I felt like she was sent to help, and I agreed. She not only took some amazing photos, she got us two backstage passes to go meet the performers!

Lily got to meet each of the idols and talk to most of them, and one, Scotty, remembered her from a Nashville trip. Pia was amazing, in all aspects of the word—sweet, beautiful, precious, caring. I could go on and on. It was just a perfect night, one to remember forever.

## National Anthem

*"…and the home of the brave!"*

Lily's beautiful voice rose as she wrapped up singing the National Anthem. Her face went from so-serious concentration to exploding in a smile that lit up the ballpark.

Lily had just opened an Atlanta Braves game against the Pittsburgh Pirates in front of a packed stadium of fans. There were few dry eyes in the house; I was certainly a teary mess. Three hundred friends and family in a nosebleed section were going crazy, but some forty thousand other people were all incredibly moved by the bravest person in the stadium. I saw our new friends from the American Idol concert, who so kindly let us use two of their tickets—they'd driven back to Atlanta from Auburn just to see Lily sing! My eyes filled with new tears as we waved to them.

People often admire athletes who overcome career-threatening injuries, saluting their bravery, but I don't think it is any stretch to say that two teams of strong, young men were blown away by the courage of my little, stick-thin girl.

But I'm not talking about her courage to get up in front of so many people—that was the easy part for her. Lily was not a bit nervous. Before the game, I tried to coach her to stay calm and focus on just one spot. "Mom," she said, bringing me up short, "stop."

I started up again, "No, look, there are a lot of people here. I want you to focus on one spot, and don't—"

"Mom, put in my earplugs, please. I've got this," Lily said, brimming with quiet confidence. Just like that—an ordinary day, singing the National Anthem in front of forty thousand people and on national television to I don't know how many more!

I put in her earplugs so she didn't hear the echo, and we walked out there.

*Lily singing the National Anthem at the Atlanta Braves Game, July 2011.*

Of course, she nailed it. Got the longest standing ovation in Brave's *history*. The applause and cheering just went on and on, and she stood there, smiling.

Here's the craziest part—total insanity. This strong, confident little girl had just taken her chemo maybe thirty minutes before singing the National Anthem. It was an oral treatment, but it had to be at a very specific time—the doctors had been on me to ensure Lily got it at exactly the right time.

And these things make you feel *horrible*.

My little trooper not only took her meds but walked onto the diamond to bang out the National Anthem like a complete and total professional, the smile on her face belying the torture going on within her body.

The next day, my phone was ringing nonstop! People were calling from all over, and Lily's brave, smiling face was on the lead page on Yahoo.com. My heart was ready to burst with pride, but Lily just took it all in stride.

"Mom, why can't I have a Facebook?" she asked.

"Because you're not going to have a Facebook," I told her. "You have a fan page." It was blowing up—from two thousand to over fifteen thousand people. The number just kept on going! Three different TV stations wanted to interview her on the air, and on the radio, they asked her to sing a Taylor Swift song. Within a week, she was a little celebrity.

Lily loved it.

In public, on TV, she was all smiles and strength and optimism. But we knew what she was going through. At home it wasn't always smiles—though she was always so strong. She was in pain, and tears flowed too.

There were times when she would just cry and say, "I don't want to do this anymore!"

I watched how sick the treatments made her, and while I can't fully fathom what she went through, I understood with a mother's heart. My only other experience with cancer was my grandfather, who was ninety-two. He got cancer, and that was it—he wasn't on chemo for three years, enduring the constant side effects of the medicine that was both making Lily sick and hopefully saving her life.

Lily was so strong—she just wanted to take the chemo and get it over with, then go do something else. Her determination and strength were utterly amazing.

# 11

# The Beauty of Normal

You may have picked up this book because you're going through something similar to what we did. Your family may be fighting for the life of a loved one...or of a marriage. I know how hard it is, how the pain just gets bigger and bigger. You may find it tempting to think of just calling it quits because you think you can't take it anymore—you might think the nightmare will stop if you give up.

If that's you, let me tell you something from a person who has been there. When you quit saying "YES" to life, death has already won—even if you're still walking, breathing, and talking.

Joey and I did everything in our power to keep looking for ways to say yes to life, even when things began to look grim. It certainly wasn't easy, but when faced with a choice between death and life, we chose life.

## Our "Normal"

The weeks after the American Idol concert and singing the National Anthem were anticlimactic—mostly in a good way.

Summer that year was pretty good, but Lily looked forward to getting back to school, seeing old friends more, and making new ones. Her best buddy, Sophie, would be with her in homeroom again for the second year—two of nine girls with *twenty* boys! I couldn't believe she was in the fifth grade already! Little Audrey started Pre-K, too, so I suddenly had afternoons alone to contend with.

I love the crazy monotony of a school-day morning, coaxing Lily to get up. The normalcy was thrilling! Homework, cheerleading, and voice lessons—the normalcy of it, the mundane details, were wonderful to me.

But at the same time, I experienced something very strange: separation anxiety. I struggled for months wondering what was wrong with me, unable to get on a schedule or get myself organized. My focus was scattered, and I wanted to scream all the time.

I had been doing a little work here and there, but my mind couldn't stay focused. All I could do was think about Lily and worry about her. I missed Lily if she was away from me; I felt like a two year old who is leaving Mommy for the first time every time she was away from me.

Don't get me wrong—I loved that she was living like a normal fifth grader, but I was still jealous of her every second. I was afraid of missing something. It was so crazy. I secretly didn't want her to go anywhere. At night, I went into her room to watch her sleep. Most nights, I got into the bed with her and kind of spooned if I could, just careful not to wake her.

I know this may sound selfish, but I yearned for her to need me like I needed her. I asked God every single night (after thanking Him first) to please leave her here on earth. She was impacting millions of people, I'd tell Him, and we need her here to change the world. "Father, Lily is changing the world, she is touching lives, please let her stay here for ninety more years."

I prayed it, but I didn't know what the answer would be. I wanted to have unwavering faith; I had dented, iron determination that she *would* live. But we faced reminders that sometimes our prayers are not answered the way we think.

## Lacrosse

Lily was invited to sing the National Anthem at a high school girls' lacrosse game. She had never met any of the students before, and they were really giving to her—a lacrosse stick, a pink t-shirt, and other items.

But the connection didn't end with Lily singing the National Anthem. These girls *loved* Lily! They would come visit her all the time at our house, and what young girl *wouldn't* want to hang out with high school girls? They adopted her as one of their own.

During this time, she was getting sicker and sicker. They made such a big deal about her—dedicating games to her and urging one another on with a cheer. They'd say, "Play for Lily! Stay strong for Lily!"

What surprised me so much was that these were high school girls. I can remember well what I was like in high school, and I only wish that I were as giving and loving as these girls were to my Lily. They made a great deal of difference in our lives, and it didn't stop there.

When Lily sang the National Anthem at the Atlanta Braves game, she received the longest standing ovation in their history. This girls' lacrosse team played that recording before every one of their home lacrosse games. They also give away a $1,000 scholarship to the senior who has the most courage.

It's the Lily Anderson Courage Award.

## Recording

Lily had the chance to record with this amazing young artist, Matt Kabus. He's an amazing artist, and he was in college at the time. He was working on a project, and a woman who saw Lily sing the National Anthem for the Braves game and was directing the project put them together.

Matt was doing a performance for the Georgia Aquarium at a Ted Turner gala. So because he was away to college, they had to do their rehearsals via Skype. He would play the guitar, and there would be a delay; then she would sing. It was neat to see them become musical computer buddies!

Later, Lily got to meet Matt and record with him before performing at the Aquarium for Ted Turner. Truly it was an amazing experience!

Lily also performed with him at an event called Children of Fallen Patriots, where children who have lost a parent in war receive some love and financial help. She sang the National Anthem again here, along with *Proud to Be An American*.

Lily made a real impression on Matt, as well, and he later wrote a song about Lily that is incredibly moving. He talks about how she taught him how to sing and perform, though she was so young. He was just so good to her!

## Difficult Questions

We continued the fight against our enemy, now at home more for chemo, which is a mixed blessing. She took the meds at night so she can sleep off the nausea, but because Lily had become conditioned to thinking she was going to throw up from the chemo, she couldn't swallow the pill. We had to break it up and put it in applesauce, and instead of getting it over with in seconds, we took twenty minutes to get it down one bite at a time.

Another grimmer aspect of our reality is that another little boy we met while fighting cancer lost his own battle. We met Bo when Lily was first diagnosed, and we loved his motto, "Be strong—be Bo strong!" It was very difficult to tell Lily that he'd died, because she was so smart and understood too much. She'd picked him to get a Wish from Kingdom Kids through "Lily's Run" and couldn't understand why he'd died and was very sad that he didn't get his wish.

I hated seeing the look of fear in her eyes when we told her about Bo, and she had to see my fear too. As smart as she was, she just couldn't wrap her head around it—who could!—and understand why her friends were dying. Then, she asked me the question that *no parent should ever have to hear from her baby*: "Mommy, am I going to die?"

I didn't know how to respond, so I was just silent for a moment and pulled her close. Tears ran down my face as I explained to her that everyone dies eventually but that we don't know exactly when.

It was a dark reminder of the stakes in this war we're fighting, and Joey, who was traveling a lot at this time, and I vowed again that we would never, ever—*ever*—give up.

## Two-year Anniversary

*At "Lily's Run" 2011, right at the two-year mark.*
*Top, Left to Right: Audrey and Lily. Bottom, Left to Right: Jennifer and Joey.*

September marked two years since Lily was diagnosed with cancer. I learned that every day, forty-six families learn their children have cancer. We participated in Change for a Change, doing whatever we could to raise money to fight this horrible disease.

People emptied piggy banks, sold bikes, and even tried to sell a little sister (Lily). It was all for such a good cause!

We had more scans in September, too, and we were all so anxious to learn the results. Going to the hospital for the tests, poor Lily threw up the moment we pulled into the parking lot. She threw up a few more times before they were even able to scan her.

Hours went by with me eyeing the phone, afraid to answer in case it was bad news. I tried to prepare myself. If they said, "Hello, Mrs. Anderson. What are you doing?" I knew we were in for bad news. If they said, "Hello, how are you?" I knew it would be good.

Our sweet nurse Elisha called and asked, "Hello, how are you?" My heart was racing, and tears were flowing. *Please God*, I prayed, *let it be good news!*

No new lesions (cancer), and the spots appeared to be getting smaller! I was so excited, I forgot to thank her and hung up to spread the good news and warm up for some cartwheels.

## Singing with Collective Soul

In early September, I got a phone call asking if Lily would sing for a fund-raiser for Ian's Friends Foundation, raising money to fight pediatric brain tumors. She was supposed to sing *The Climb* with Christopher Alan Yates. Getting ready for the event, we got to go to Ed Roland's house—lead singer of Collective Soul—who actually lives in Atlanta.

We got to meet the band members the day of the event, and lead singer Ed asked her if she wanted to sing with them. "Yes!" she replied enthusiastically.

"What song do you want to sing?" he asked her.

She didn't hesitate: "SHINE of course!" and then started belting out the song! Ed joined her after a moment, creating the most amazing memory. She had never rehearsed the song with Ed or the band before this day—the plan was just to sing *The Climb* with Christopher Alan Yates. Collective Soul would be the next performance.

I remember Ed just looking at her with a funny expression and saying, "I'll tell you when to come in—"

"Mr. Roland," Lily interrupted. "I wanted to sing the entire song. By myself." He went from unsure to white-faced as he processed. We all laughed at my precocious Lily telling Ed Roland, lead singer of the amazing band Collective Soul, how it was going to be!

Finally, he smiled. "Of course you're going to sing the whole thing!"

I'm pretty sure that actually singing with the band for the event was bigger, though. She sang her theme song, *The Climb*, with new friend Christopher, and they let her sing the entire song *Shine* by herself! She'd never rehearsed with them, and it's their number one song. Ed let her do the whole song, and she completely killed it!

*Lily singing with Collective Soul.*

## Challenge

With every day so precious, it really hammered home that we don't have any time to waste on this earth—none of us! One day while driving Lily to school, I told her that she needed to make someone feel good that day. It was her "Challenge."

On the way home that afternoon after cheerleading, I asked her how it went. She said that she had complimented a new friend in class that day—and the little girl happened to be in the car with us!

"Would you challenge her every day, Mrs. Anderson?" she asked. So cute!

What would our world be like if we all lived like we weren't guaranteed a tomorrow? What would it be like if we all accepted the challenge to make someone's day better?

I challenge you like I challenged Lily—make a difference today. Go pick up someone's lunch. Help an elderly person pump gas. Carry someone's groceries. Hug your kids for long enough they try to get away—and fail!

Lily taught me to live every day to its fullest, and I hope that you will learn this lesson as well.

# 1 2

# No Stone Unturned

Lily lived so much *life*. She was so engaged, so full of wonder and delight. Doors opened for incredible experiences, and Lily touched lives. We reveled in our normalcy of school and voice lessons and hard work. We counted ourselves so lucky to do things like sing with Collective Soul and record a commercial for the Atlanta Braves. Christmas was a time of incredible rejoicing, and we rang in 2012 with a lot of optimism.

Then something happened to take my breath away and leave a gnawing pit in my stomach. In late March, Lily started to complain of leg pain again. I, of course, freaked out, and Joey remained calm, making us a great pair. After obsessing and crying through the weekend, Lily's doctor had us schedule another scan to see what we were dealing with.

The results were confusing and not what we wanted to hear. Because the MIBG scan does not work with Lily, we had to have PET scans. Lily would drink a liquid called "contrast," and then they would inject her port with a substance that would light up any areas with activity. Lily's cancer in her pelvis area had changed over the months, not so much the size of the spot, but the amount of uptake that area was absorbing.

We weren't sure what to make of the news, but we knew we didn't want to tell her that we might have to change her treatment routine. While we waited to meet with the doctors and discuss our options, we were in a holding pattern.

It made me so *mad!* I was exhausted and overwhelmed with fear, frustrated that I couldn't do a thing to stop this monster. Enough was enough! We wanted off this crazy roller coaster! While I reacted, Joey kept a level head and pointed out there could be any number of reasons for the scan to "light up" more.

I hoped he was right, and when Lily went to school with no leg pain, I tried to not let the inconclusive scan bring me down. I tried to stay calm, not panic—*ha!*—and ask smart questions of the doctors. With her leg pain coming and going, Lily left them scratching their heads and joking that if they lost all their hair, she'd be the reason!

## Trouble

In May, we had a MRI on Lily's leg to see why she was having pain there. Unfortunately, the scan showed that Lily's medicine was no longer working. We would have to switch up again. We researched different options, and we found a trial in Atlanta that seemed like a good fit. I couldn't decide if I should pray that we got in—she had to "qualify" by being at a certain place with her cancer—or that she was "too healthy" for the program!

We also went through a hospital marathon, where Lily endured about a thousand tests (actually about seven), including an echocardiogram, blood work, a physical, another PET scan, and even a bone marrow aspirate (ugh!) all in one day. Her best friend, Sophie, came with us—who was a lifesaver—and we tried to take our minds off of it by playing "Where's Sophie?" Just like "Where's Waldo?" Sophie would be in some part of the hospital we were in. I'd take a picture, and then we'd laugh hysterically trying to find Sophie in the picture. We were in the hospital for upwards of twelve hours, and everywhere we went, Sophie would get into the picture somehow.

The worst part might have been that Lily couldn't eat anything *all day!* We started at seven in the morning and didn't leave till after five. Lily graciously gave us permission to sneak off, one by one, to get a snack—while she sat drinking contrast for her PET scan. We told her we got flat, warm Coke and stale, old potato chips, which got an eye roll.

Being unsure of what was going on in Lily's leg and if what we were doing was helping was utter torture. We tried to take our minds off of it with a trip to the beach in the middle of June, but even though she was an incredibly brave little girl, her leg pain was just too much for her. She spent the entire trip on pain meds, but nothing with Tylenol, because her liver enzymes were out of whack.

We prayed that the new combination of drugs would do the trick. Just their names, so hard to pronounce and frighteningly clinical, were intimidating. Why couldn't they be called something nicer? For once, I would have liked to hear a nurse say, "Today Lily will be getting Daisy Petals mixed with Glitter Icing!"

The treatment was a combination of oral meds, which she now took every single day, and infusions in the hospital. Honestly, she did well with it, with only a yucky tummy at times.

Despite all of this, we let her go to summer camp, which she *loved*. She stayed with eleven other girls in a cabin for five nights. I missed her incredibly and worried constantly. But I was glad to hear what a great time she'd had when she got back and started sharing all her stories.

## Horrible Words

It was now July 2012. As the weeks went on, Lily was in constant pain and seemed to be getting worse; it was utter torture to watch my child be in such pain. The new chemotherapy didn't seem to be working, and we were confronted by the possibility we'd need to try something else. Not only that, I saw something different in Lily's demeanor—she told me that if she lost her hair again, she wanted to be homeschooled. She didn't want to go to middle school in a bandana, but she had always loved school and her friends so much. I hoped and prayed this didn't indicate a loss of heart for the fight.

Things got even more complicated when her liver enzymes went up again and we couldn't do her chemotherapy with the elevated levels. A couple of ultrasounds later (no one told us she couldn't eat before the first one!) and we had no more answers, just mounting worries and questions. They took us to the same conference room we'd gone to when Lily was first diagnosed.

The doctor pulled up images on his computer and showed us Lily's pelvis. The new scans showed that Lily had tumors all up and down her pelvis. Joey and I were completely devastated.

"It's bad," Dr. Rapkin said. "I think it's time we consider hospice."

"No," I said back, sharply. "We're fine." Joey wanted facts, and I wanted more options. He wanted to know exactly what we were dealing with, but my mind was just in a fog. Finally, Joey asked how much longer she had.

"Mr. and Mrs. Anderson, Lily has six to eight weeks to live— probably." I could see that Dr. Rapkin hated delivering this news. "There's nothing more we can do."

*Nothing more we can do…*

It was like the words were in another language and I had to translate them into English with difficulty. We both fell apart, sobbing. I felt like the train had derailed, and I wasn't strong enough to fix it. Things had gone wildly, horribly out of control.

As my tears paused, a new, instinctive reaction rose up in me.

*No.*

There may be nothing else *they* could do, but *we* were not done. We were *not* giving up, no matter what.

I began to dive into research, looking for anything—any ray of hope, any option. I read about drugs and their side effects. I was determined to leave no stone unturned, no matter how far I had to look or what we had to do. We had to keep going; there was something out there, I was sure. We just had to find it…

My research led me to something, a glimmer—a treatment in England that the FDA hadn't approved in the U.S. They were doing it for neuroblastoma patients, and five out of six kids were doing better after the treatment. This could be it! The next morning, Joey physically carried Lily into the post office to get a passport made. We drew a lot of looks, because Lily was too weak to walk. People stared at us, all around—but this was nothing new. People were always staring.

We were going to go to England.

I didn't even know how hard a journey across the Atlantic would be for Lily, in her current condition, but it was the best hope we had.

But after many hours of research, suddenly I learned of something else—a clinic in Houston, Texas, where a doctor had begun using this treatment…on adults. I called them immediately: "I have an eleven-year-old girl, and she needs this treatment. I need you to do it on my daughter. It's life or death!"

"I'm sorry, she's too young," they replied. "We have no FDA approval."

I was undeterred. "Well, how do I get FDA approval?" I asked. They told me in some broad strokes. "I'm going to start with my local congressman, and then I'm going up the ladder *until I get FDA approval*," I told them with finality.

I was like a crazy person, a woman possessed—with a single idea. *Life.*

Even before we knew what would happen with the FDA, we headed to Houston to the clinic to get some tests done, not even knowing if she was going to be able to have the treatment. But I wanted everything lined up, so we were paying out of our pocket because the insurance wouldn't cover the tests. They injected Lily with something and then scanned her to see if it would go to the cancer cells in her body. After several scans…we learned Lily was a candidate for the treatment!

Just one little hurdle: the FDA.

Dr. Delpassand, who ran the clinic, wanted to do the treatment for Lily because he loved her from the first time he met her, like everyone else. But you had to be at least eighteen for him to do it.

I just told him, "I'm going to figure it out."

And then I got on the phone. I called and called—and called. Dr. Delpassand called. We talked to anyone and everyone we could think of.

I was going to do anything in my power to make it happen, so when Dr. Delpassand told me that I needed to call the FDA myself. I got on the phone with the FDA in Virginia, right outside Washington, DC, trying to talk anyone I could into helping us. I pleaded our case, begged.

Would it be enough? We couldn't know…we could just keep trying. We needed a miracle. I can't even describe the fear I felt, wondering if Lily would get this chance at life.

## Miracles Do Happen

I will never forget the moment it happened. Dr. Delpassand came running down the hallway of his clinic. My heart stopped in my chest as he took a second to catch his breath. Lily and I were worn out—she was crying, because the nurse had just taken her IV out because they had missed her veins several times trying to get it in and she was very sore.

But through my haze, I heard words I'd been praying to hear with everything in me: "We got it!" he said—shouted. "We got it!" I had called at 3:00 p.m., and it was just now 3:30 p.m., Tuesday, July 31st.

We had approval! I was stunned—we'd done it! Lily would be the first child in the U.S. to get this new treatment. It was a miracle! We had the first treatment the next day, and despite her throwing up a lot because of some amino acids they gave her to protect her kidneys, the results seemed nearly immediate.

But that was just the first, and smallest, miracle we needed.

## Radioactive

By this point, Lily could not walk well because of the tumors. She was in a wheelchair, and it was very painful. My mom, Lily's best friend Sophie, and I had all gone with her to Houston to help, and it was an intense but encouraging time now that we had approval and could move forward with the treatments.

The medicine was crazy—LU-177 it was called, and it was literally radioactive material that they fed into my baby's body intravenously. It was horrible, crazy—we were intentionally irradiating our baby! But it would stop cancer cells, attack them.

We had to be in a specially approved hotel that could handle situations like this with radioactive material. They had to be able to cleanse the room, and they'd worked with the hospitals before. Lily's room was connected to ours, but she had to have her own suite, and I couldn't sleep with her and had to be careful. We couldn't go within six feet of her for two days, she was so radioactive! The IV made her very sick...but hopefully it was killing the cancer.

So she got this first, horrible miracle treatment, and after we were finished, we were able to head back home. Back in Atlanta, they did some scans. I don't know if I breathed.

It was shrinking!

She started walking better. Then running! She had to go back for more treatments, but her goal was to be back and ready for the start of school—the sixth grade.

Having been told our daughter had six to eight weeks to live in July, by August she was walking down the hallway of her school, getting ready to start sixth grade! We had decorated her locker before we left for Houston, and her hope was a powerful thing, motivating her through the frightening radioactive treatments. She and Sophie would be in the same homeroom, and while Lily was still on crutches, Sophie carried her books.

But when Lily came back, she wasn't on crutches! She wasn't just walking, either—she was running!

# 1 3

# Baby Steps to Climb a Mountain

Oh, the joy of those weeks after the treatment in Houston! Lily was a different child since the end of July when things were going so badly. We left Atlanta with Lily in a wheelchair, and days later she was swimming before cheerleading practice. Lily lived as much life in her years as many people do in a lifetime, and we were all simply enjoying being alive in the weeks after this miracle treatment in Houston.

She had regained her determination to make it back to school, and it had driven her despite radioactive treatments, chemo, and the persistent sick, horrible feeling that came with the "medicine."

We had new hope, and the crazy normalcy of school helped with that. Lily was starting middle school and Audrey was starting kindergarten. It was an exciting time! I say "exciting," but it was also bittersweet: my baby was off to kindergarten, and my hero was braving middle school. I was a bit overwhelmed by all the preparation for those first days of school. Ironic, isn't it? I talked the FDA into approving an experimental procedure for an eleven year old, but getting ready for the first day of school seemed like too much!

Lily wanted an early wake-up call so she would have plenty of time to get ready for school. Audrey had slept in sponge rollers so her hair would be curly in the morning. Both girls had arranged their outfits on the floor so they would know exactly how they would look in the morning, and the morning blitz to get both ready saw me frantically trying to snap a few pictures I never managed to post.

Looking back, I fear that Lily's fight with cancer often overshadowed Audrey and her adventures in life. She was so little when Lily got sick, and fighting the monster seemed to take up so much of our energy. The wonder and beauty of a few "firsts" may have gotten lost in the shuffle, but she was always such a bright light in our family!

I hadn't expected her first day of kindergarten to be overly dramatic, but this was my baby—it turned out to be more dramatic than I expected! (But not for Audrey.) Let me paint you a picture: Joey held one hand and I held Audrey's other hand as we walked down what seemed like the longest hallway in history. Audrey was skipping with excitement, and her adorable teacher greeted us at the door and told Audrey she could sit wherever she wanted.

As the rest of the class arrived, it was obvious how well Audrey fit in. It's like she had been doing this for months already! For some reason, though, I was having trouble with it all. Maybe it was too easy?

I secretly wanted Audrey to get up and run over to us, screaming, "No, don't leave!" But instead she dove into a book and only looked up for a second as I said, "Bye, Audrey, I love you!"

Her teacher guided us to the door and told us that she would call to give us a full report on the day, and Joey and I snapped plenty of pictures. Just as we turned to go down the hallway, Joey darted back into the room for more pictures! It was so precious; his little buddy was embarking on a new adventure, and he was as nervous as I was! The teacher ushered him out again, and now together but feeling strangely alone, we headed down that hallway for the longest walk ever.

Would she miss us? Would she cry when she really realized we were gone? What if the other kids were mean to her? What if she got on the wrong bus heading home?

I had a knot in my throat but realized how confident and amazing our little Audrey was. I had two little heroes! I remember getting into the car and seeing that Joey looked like I felt.

"No more baby Audrey," he said. "She's a big girl now."

Dropping Lily off at school was very different. She had grown up so fast! Sophie drove with us to this first day of middle school. Both girls were dressed to impress. As Sophie jumped out, her brand-new shiny backpack somehow hooked Audrey's booster seat!

I called out, feeling like I was stuck in slow motion: "Sooooophie!" But before I could get it out, she'd gotten outside the car...with the booster hanging from her backpack. The kicker is that *she didn't know it!* Sophie's so fun—this is just her. Lily couldn't stop laughing—and she'd laugh hysterically every time we told that story!

While we were sitting in the carpool drop-off line, I had asked Lily, "Can I still get a kiss before you jump out of the car?"

She smiled. "Yes, Mommy—but quick before we get to the school door!"

"Bye, Lily… I love you!" I told her.

"Love you too!" And then she was gone.


## A Mass

What a difference two weeks make. Just two weeks ago I was dropping Lily off to school. Two weeks ago, things were normal—first day of school jitters, for Mom.

It seemed like I blinked and the dream of "normal" was over. Lily woke up with a very bad headache and her leg also hurting. By the end of the day, she was violently throwing up and the pain had gotten to a "ten" out of ten.… That was a Saturday, and by Sunday morning she could hardly raise her head up and the vomiting had not stopped. She said she was seeing double, sometimes triple.

We headed to the emergency room where they gave Lily some pain meds and after a CT scan said that she just had a "migraine."

And then they sent us home.

The next couple days were horrible; her head still pounded, and she wouldn't eat anything. As soon as we could, we got in for a MRI of her head because of the continuing vision problems and headaches.

Many hours later... We received devastating news.

Lily had a mass at the base of her skull, sitting on her optic nerve.

Many tears later... We were rushed into radiation to start hitting this mass immediately. They were afraid that if we didn't start right away, Lily could lose her eyesight!

One of Lily's many friends was especially amazing at this time. Rhett, an incredible friend whom Lily loved, told me, "Miss Jen, would you come pick me up so I can go to radiation with you and Lily?"

Every morning we went for radiation, we'd go pick him up at 5:00 a.m. He had a bag of Honey Nut Cheerios to share with Lily, and he'd ride with us the hour it took to get there, the time it took to get the treatment (the treatments themselves only took around ten minutes) and then the hour back. He had to be at school by 7:30, and we'd drop him off at school. He got up more than two hours early every time we had a treatment just because he loved Lily so much.

We had ten rounds of radiation planned, and after the second one Lily woke up one morning and wanted to go to school.

God, how I loved hearing that!

## Bittersweet

Wrestling with this new discovery was difficult. Mixed in with those days was an incredible act of love and friendship as my friend, Shannon, stole my password to an amazing website called Care Pages and posted about our financial needs. The response of love and support was nothing short of a miracle! The costs for the treatments in Houston were considerable, and because of Shannon's initiative to con me out of my password and share our need, individuals in the community responded in a way that brought tears of joy to eyes that had known only tears of sadness for too long.

Also, September found us recognizing that three years ago Joey and I received our "membership cards" to battling childhood cancer. We could not decide whether to be happy that our little girl, who had received such a dire prognosis, was still fighting— or to be horrified that we had been in this hellish war for three whole years....

In the end we decided not to dwell on it, because we figured the cancer would just love it if it found out it had made us upset!

We had another treatment in Houston planned, but Lily had to be healthy enough to go, so I continued to live in anxiety. Little blessings like mysterious gas cards showing up in our mailbox helped take the edge off, and we tried to keep a good attitude and trust God.

The flight back to Houston for her second treatment was very difficult for Lily because she was in such pain. She was also very tired, both physically and emotionally. The disease was all in her pelvis area, rubbing on the nerves and bones. She was not able to walk again, and my appreciation for those who care for a loved one in a wheelchair grew. I had no idea how much work it could be to get someone in and out of the chair, get into a car, and just drive down the road before repeating the process to go home.

The second treatment in Houston was easier on Lily than the first, and instead of throwing up the whole day, she was just nauseated and miserable. The next day we went back in for another scan to see if the medicine was working. Her pelvis area lit up, as did a small spot at the back of her head. In a way, this was a good thing—we did not know what type of tumor she had there. To my untrained eye, it looked as though the radiation had shrunk it, but we would not be sure until we got back to Atlanta for another MRI.

Shannon went with us, which was such a huge blessing, not the least of which was because the Rita Foundation fund-raising efforts she had started had received almost enough money to pay for the treatments in Houston!

## Baby Steps

The second trip to Houston was more painful for Lily—and for me. Shannon and I could *see* a difference in her. She was not her typically upbeat self as often. Was she losing the war of the mind? She'd been fighting for so long.... Was our precious Lily losing out to the monster inside? Was it eating away at her personality as well as her body? The thought filled me with a different kind of fear.

The second treatment seemed to make a small bit of difference, but she still could not walk. While the first one had left her walking for about three weeks, even running and jumping, it didn't last. After, her symptoms got worse and worse. If the first one had been such a miracle (even for a moment) what did it say that the second hadn't had as much apparent effect?

I was definitely not looking forward to meeting with her doctor back in Atlanta. Part of me wanted to just bury my head in the sand and pretend everything would be okay. I did not want another doctor telling me one more bad thing about Lily! I knew the symptoms were not a good sign, but I did not know if I could bear to hear any bad news.

But instead of bad news, the scans revealed that the tumors were in fact shrinking. I could hardly believe it, but even to my eyes they *did* look smaller! Also, the doctor told us that it was possible the new medicine was inflaming a tumor that had already been present in Lily's skull, causing her headaches and blurred vision.

The doctor was cautiously optimistic; he felt that the new treatments were attacking the cancer and that Lily would start to feel better little by little. We would be heading back to Houston by the end of October, so we hoped that Lily would feel good enough to go back to school between returning to Atlanta and then.

At least that was our hope. I didn't know how I felt right then; afraid *not* to hope, but filled with fears. The best thing I could do was pray.

We'd exhausted just about every other option.

# 1 4

# Downhill Slide

After the results from our first treatment in Houston, where Lily arrived in a wheelchair and returned to Atlanta running and jumping, our disappointment after the second treatment's limited improvement was crushing. The doctor's cautious optimism leaked away as the days progressed. In fact, she saw little if any improvement after the second round.

We returned from Houston on a Saturday, and by Sunday Lily seemed obviously going downhill. Tuesday morning she woke up completely soaked in sweat, and we rushed to the ER. Her blood counts were low and she would need a transfusion—which she had not needed for over two years. They admitted us, and Lily was definitely not happy about that!

A CT scan showed that her intestines and colon were inflamed, and we called the doctors in Houston to see if this may be a known side effect. It was not, but the drugs went to areas with cancer and inflamed them. As far as we knew, Lily did not have any cancer in her intestines and colon… Had that changed?

Two days later they discharged us, but they had Lily on an IV of antibiotics and fluids, which a nurse showed me how to administer right into her port. The difference Shannon and I noticed in her on the last trip to Houston was more pronounced, and Lily was very sad and just wanted to get back to her normal self. That, of course, was our prayer from the beginning.

Nowhere was this more evident than how we left the hospital. When given the chance to choose between staying in the hospital to get the antibiotics or returning home, Lily flipped out at the doctor and proceeded to go on a tirade. She did not want her port accessed at home because it was embarrassing—she didn't want Audrey to see it. She couldn't sleep, she hated the hospital, and she hated Dr. George! All of these feelings came out in about two seconds, and I stumbled out of the room with tears streaming down my face, letting her duke it out with him.

Then I heard her say, "FORGET IT... I AM NOT LEAVING THIS HOSPITAL WITH THIS ACCESS! WE ARE STAYING HERE! I AM NOT GOING TO EAT ANYTHING IN THIS PLACE, I WON'T DRINK ANYTHING FROM THIS PLACE, AND WE WILL STAY HERE UNTIL I AM FINISHED WITH THIS STUPID ANTIBIOTIC!"

There was total silence while I tried to choke down my tears so she would not hear me. After about a minute, I gathered myself and stormed back into the battle. "We are not staying in this hospital," I told her. "We are going home, because as smart as you are, I still know better than you do." I softened my tone then. "You will feel better in your own bed at home."

I won the fight, but my understanding of where my precious Lily was mentally had shaken me to the core. No matter how difficult her treatments, she had never acted like this before. I was terrified of what it meant.

No child should ever have to go through this nightmare. Lily was so sad about missing school and her friends, being unable to go to cheerleading, run, or jump. She just wanted to be a normal kid! And our desperate prayer for her was that she could be. But "normal" wasn't in the cards we were dealt; we just had to do the best with what we had.

## Up and Down

The next few weeks were definitely a mixed bag. For a while, Lily did very well and had a good week—she even made it to school for part of the week! Then she started to complain of pain on her head; not like a headache, but soreness on her scalp. It didn't appear to be a burn from radiation, but we just didn't know.

The pain in her leg was also up and down. One day she was walking the halls of her school, and the next she was in bed, unable to walk.

The fourth annual "Lily's Run" was in October, and it had always been such an uplifting time. This time, I wasn't so sure. The day after it, we would be returning to Houston for more tests. The plan was that we would return to Atlanta just long enough to kiss Joey and Audrey before flying back to Houston near the end of October for a third round of treatments.

Unfortunately, she needed to be well enough to travel, and a week into October, we were back in the hospital for another platelet transfusion. Lily went from pale and fragile to looking sun-kissed, with ruby red lips within just a few hours. She was able to sleep through most of it, but my friend Shannon and I were not. We were so delirious with exhaustion that we laughed at everything, trying hard not to wake Lily up.

Despite a lasting fever from a virus that she contracted while her blood counts were so low, Lily felt well enough to attend the fourth annual "Lily's Run." It went perfectly! She was healthy enough to travel, too, though our trip to Houston was filled with tests and scans. It was made more difficult by the fact that Lily was just…not herself. She missed school and friends in cheerleading and voice lessons so much. It was just too much for an eleven year old to understand! It was too hard for her forty-something-year-old Mom to understand, too.

All the tests and scans were draining, but the upshot was that her platelet count was too low and we had to postpone her third treatment till November. I had really wanted to get it over with, but I don't think that her little body could handle any more just then. The pain in her legs was just awful. She couldn't walk, and when she did try, she was bent over like a crippled old woman. Every time I saw it, my heart shattered and I swept her up into my arms to carry her where she needed to go. Her little body felt so thin and light in my arms… I tried not to think about it.

Joey and I were bleary-eyed from lack of sleep. As October drew to a close, the pain was so bad that even with pain medication Lily was in tears from just trying to move. We tried to keep it under control with meds and warm baths, but it was just too much. Our hearts were breaking in our chests in a spiritual pain that mirrored her every cry and tear.

In the middle of all this, life continued on, with Audrey losing her first tooth. We tried to make it a big deal for her, but it was such a struggle to put on a happy face. Her spunk and energy were like transfusions for our hearts the same way Lily's were, precious lifeblood to a family desperately in need of infusions of joy. Just talking to her made me happy and was one of the few bright points during this time—I'm not sure she understood how awesome she was in handling all that was going on around her. A whole other section of my heart hurts that she never knew her sister BC (before cancer). I didn't know if my heart could break more than it already was because of Lily's pain, but it broke a little more when I thought about that.

Audrey always woke up in a happy mood, a morning person just like me! I loved how she bounced out of bed, ready to start the day. Her energy was infectious!

## Denial

My little hero could not seem to rebound from the last round of medicine, and her blood counts stayed low for many weeks. She was in a lot of pain and had difficulty eating because the pain took her appetite away. We went in for transfusion after transfusion, making me so incredibly grateful for all the people who donate blood.

I was broken as I watched my baby cry in pain...with no control over fixing it for her.

We got a bit of a respite for Thanksgiving, and thanks to a transfusion and platelets, she had a better holiday. I was thrilled to have a dose of normal, at least for a few hours anyway. She even felt good enough to go to Joey's mom's and sat at the table with us. She ate a tiny bit of green beans, corn, and turkey, but I was just glad that she was upright! We had also figured out a method with her medicines that seemed to keep the pain under control, but I hated it that she was on such heavy drugs all the time.

A difficult reality check hit me when I drove to the tag office to get an official handicap tag for my car. I was sick the entire ride and almost in denial; I didn't want that tag in my car, because it meant that I had a wheelchair in the back of my car—like I was accepting that Lily couldn't walk, and wouldn't. I cried while talking to the clerk at the tag agency, and I cried on the way home. I stuck the tag down in the pocket of the door so I wouldn't see it.

But it was still there.

## Lanterns For Lily

Christmas is closing in, and our family had a lot of help celebrating with "Lanterns for Lily," where a special "elf" friend came out in December to light eleven paper lanterns in front of our house (one for each year of Lily's life). Lily's cheerleading coach, April, had come up with this amazing idea. All of the lanterns had special notes on them for Lily, and I loved seeing her smiles as she read them. Our special friends put so much love into each and every lantern!

I found out that Walmart and Target had such a run on paper lanterns that they couldn't keep them on the shelf! These simple white bags were sitting on shelves for months, just waiting for their chance to shine!

Word of this quickly spread, and I learned that people all over the country were lighting eleven lanterns at night for our sweet baby. I received pictures from Colorado to Connecticut to California of eleven lanterns lit in honor of Lily. It's amazing how Lily's life has impacted so many people—but it wasn't just her. This was all part of God's plan.

So many people referred to Lily as a light and encouragement to them as she struggled with her disease. It was a fun discovery to notice that her full name, LilliAN kaTE andeRsoN has "lantern" right in it! It was of course never planned, but it amazed us that people were putting out Lanterns for Lily, our little light, and she had "lantern" in her name. She was a light for so many people!

God knew way before we did that Lily would impact the world and touch thousands of lives. Her light shone brightly from the time she entered the world, and it was a light that death could not dim. At the time, it felt like that light was dimming, flickering. I was afraid it would go out forever, but that is not our eternity. When our candles go out, we have a God who will breathe them back into flame—eternal flame.

Closing in on Christmas time, I was just comforted by little representations of the Light of the World when darkness threatened to close in.

# 1 5

# Spoon Your Kids

When Lily was first diagnosed, they told us she had six months to live. How they can tell you these things, I don't know—they try to judge it by how much cancer a child has and how sick she is. But we never let that enter our minds.

Almost three years later, the doctors told us that Lily had six to eight weeks to live. They had told us that at the end of June, and she had lived another four months since that declaration. After the first treatment in Houston, things looked up. I'll never forget her running out of the school wearing little green skinny jeans! We had some really good days from July to fall.

Now Christmas was coming.

Lily had exceeded expectations again and again. My little hero had fought and fought and would not give up. Neither would I. I was determined that there was something else we could find to help her.

But not all battles can be won.

I debated ever writing this book, because at one point I thought it had only a horrible ending…

But it doesn't.

## Every Moment Counts

I could hardly bear to be apart from Lily toward the end, and in fact, I had been with her every possible moment since she got sick. I frequently slept with Lily in my arms, which made her radiation treatments difficult because I couldn't hold her.

I am a big advocate spooning with your kids. It's the coolest, because it is almost like they were back in the womb. I spooned Lily when she was little, and when she was sick. I spooned with Audrey, and poor Joey would say, "Mommy, can you sleep with me?" But he really understood, and he would tell me to go sleep next to Lily—I needed her as much as she needed comforting.

One night I was spooning with her, and I was crying because I was so exhausted from seeing the pain she was in and being so utterly helpless. The only thing I could do was give her more morphine, and even that didn't completely fix it. I was emotionally and physically at the end of my rope.

Lily must have felt me crying, and she turned her head and looked up at me. "Mom, are you crying?" she asked.

Wiping my tears, I said, "No, no. I'm not crying...."

The ghost of a sad smile crossed her face. "Mommy," she said, "stop crying. If you cry, the devil wins."

She was so young to be so deep, to have such a grasp on suffering. I couldn't understand how she was saying that to me, how she had such peace. I just knew that my little Lily was, and always will be, a hero.

# Hospice

On December 9 we had to take Lily to the emergency room—she could no longer feel her legs. From her chest down, she couldn't feel a thing. We had no idea what was going on. Lily was now too sick to go back to Houston for more treatments, so we were at home...while she became paralyzed from the chest down as the cancer climbed her spinal cord. We found out a new tumor had crushed her nerves, and she couldn't even tell if she was going to the bathroom.

I couldn't believe it. After all we had been through, after all the fighting, after the miracle of getting FDA approval for an experimental drug that seemed to make things so different...for such a short time. It was as though she had enjoyed one last, brief summer in the sun—running and jumping and *living "YES"* so abundantly.

Lily had fought past everyone's expectations, beaten the odds time and again, and had been so strong. She had lived a "YES" life!

So how could it go like this? She deserved better! She'd worked so hard, she deserved to win her fight. I could not believe that after all she'd been through...that it was over. She had fought the good fight, but they told us it was not enough.

The doctors sent us home—for hospice.

I can't decide which is the second worst day of my life: finding out Lily had cancer, or being sent home to die.

It was truly terrible, because from the chest up, Lily was normal and could talk and laugh and move her arms. It was like her lower half decided to die before the rest of her, and the contrast was jarring. She had new tumors on her scalp, little bumps under the skin where they were starting to grow.

We knew we were close to the end, and a hospice nurse came to our house to help with Lily's care. She didn't understand why the nurse was there—and I did not want her to know what it meant.

"Don't even say that word," I said. "I'm just going to tell her there is a nurse coming to the house to help me because she was so sick."

But Lily knew. Oh, yes, my precious girl knew, but she never said anything to me. She just asked who the nurse was.

"This is Suzanne," I told Lily. "She is a nurse and is going to help me."

I had already told Suzanne that she was very lucky to be taking care of such a special girl! "She's very special, and I don't care what you say—she's special!" Suzanne might have been taken aback, because I was venting at her, but then anger is not uncommon in these situations. She was a professional. You see, in a way I was mad at her. But I wasn't mad at *her*, I was angry about the whole situation.

Suzanne was with us from Sunday, the day she came, to the following Saturday.


## Volunteer

Suzanne came to help us on a Sunday, and I was scheduled to help with Audrey's kindergarten classroom the next day. I was torn about what to do, but in her special way, Lily solved my problem.

"Mom," she told me that morning, "I'm coming with you." It wasn't a question. I told her that she was too sick to come with me, but she just said, "I am going. Put me in the car—*I'm going.*"

She couldn't feel anything from the chest down, felt like crap, and yet she knew she had something to do. So I put her in the car, pale as a ghost, and drove her to a kindergarten class. Lily sat in her wheelchair and cut out shapes with Audrey, simply spending the day with her little sister in her school classroom, in her world.

She did it because she knew she was going to die, but she never told me that. We both just knew.

Lily was so brave, even with all the indignities of her condition. The school nurse had to help her, an eleven year old with a diaper, but she did not complain. She told me, "Mom, it's okay. Take me down to the nurse." She was so strong; she made the day about Audrey and spending quality time with her little sister, no matter the indignities she had to endure. And she did not say one word of complaint.

The following day Audrey came down with an ear infection, and when we got home from visiting the doctor, Lily decided to tell Audrey everything she needed to know about how to get better and how to handle being sick. She was on the couch where she spent so much of her time now. "Now, Audrey, you need to take your medicine like a big girl," she told her little sister. "You watched me always take my medicine, now you have to take your medicine for Mommy. Don't fight Mommy, just take your medicine."

It was heart wrenching to listen to her try to deliver to her little sister the most important things she had learned in her eleven years. It must've been hard for her, knowing that she was going to die, yet still wanting to be Audrey's big sister.

## Time to Let Go

They delivered a hospice bed to our house, and Lily's reaction was so classically Lily: "What's that?" she asked. I told her it was a very cool bed that would be in the living room so we did not have to carry her upstairs and downstairs. But she wasn't having any of that. "I'm not getting in that bed," she said. "That's stupid. I won't sleep in it, I'm going to stay right here on the couch."

I tried to convince her that it was awesome and exciting, but she just wanted what was familiar. She just wanted to be normal, an ordinary kid for a little while longer. She didn't want a hospice bed. If that meant that Daddy had to carry her upstairs, who cared.

Pastor Steven Gibbs from our church came to visit on Tuesday, and Lily was in her bed sleeping. He and I had a very difficult conversation…that was completely necessary.

"You have to let her go," he told me. "You have to tell her it's okay."

"I can't…."

He said, "Jennifer, she's looking for your permission, but she's not going to tell you that. She doesn't want you and Daddy to be sad anymore, or Audrey to be sad. I know that you think you're keeping stuff from her, but she knows what's going on."

I had a very difficult time even understanding him. It was like his words were not being translated into my brain, like he was speaking a foreign language that I had to try to translate before I could get them.

*Let her go? Tell her it's okay?*

We had fought this monster for so long, been strong so long. It was like I didn't understand the concept of quitting, shifting gears so that the horrible roller coaster ride could end with Lily finally having peace. We had never let the possibility that it would end this way enter our conversations and the way we lived, but ever since the doctors had said that there was no more they could do, we had all known that outside of a miracle this day would come.

Now that it was here, now that it was time to let go, it felt as though my heart simply did not know how—like stiffened fingers that had gripped something so tightly for so long that they must be pried open.

That was what Pastor Gibbs kind words did—they began to soften my grip so I could let go.

*Let go...*

"Do I have to tell her it's okay to go?" I asked him.

"Yes."

He then began to tell me about heaven, how she would get a new name from God, how a thousand years here are like only a day there. I have followed Jesus for a long time, but you simply do not think much about heaven and mortality when you are young and healthy. Pastor Gibbs' words of comfort began a slow work of healing on my heart—healing that would take a long time to come but started while we still had Lily with us.

There is no way Lily could have heard us, but as though she and Pastor Gibbs had both known it was the right time—with me the one out of the loop—the next day we had the worst conversation I had ever had *in my life*. It's as if God had set me up the day before to handle this conversation. We were on the couch, and she was feeling horrible.

She asked, "Mommy, does Daddy know I have a tumor on my spine?"

I managed to say, "Yes, Daddy knows."

"Is he sad?"

"He's devastated. He is so very, very sad...."

She said, "I love you so much, and I love Daddy and Audrey so much, but it's time for me to go." My precious hero, so much older than her years...

I couldn't find my voice, couldn't find words for what I had to say. But finally I managed, "Okay." I just kept saying over and over, "Okay, okay, okay...." I was kneeling in front of her with my head in her tiny lap and she gently stroked my hair.

## Good-bye

Lily's condition deteriorated quickly after that. I had to catheterize her three times a day with the help of my friend Wendy, a nurse, because Lily hated the hospice nurse. Wendy has a daughter named Hannah, and she and Lily were very close friends. We had to hide Suzanne behind the couch so Lily wouldn't see her! Lily was in a lot of pain, and because of the medication she was in and out.

She was so uncomfortable. Her friends desperately wanted to see her, but she could hardly bear to be seen by anyone. We had that horrible conversation about letting her go on Wednesday, and Thursday night some friends came to see her. Officially it was just a visit, but really it was to say good-bye. Lily had not wanted anybody at the house at first, and I respected that, but suddenly she said, "Mom, where's Rhett?" He was her special friend, a sweet boy.

I called his mom and asked her to get him over to our house right away. They lived really close by, so he got there quickly. Lily had been sleeping for hours, but when he got there she sat up as much as she could and raised her arms up for a big hug. The poor boy was so scared, just standing there, until his dad urged him, "Rhett, go and get that hug!" He got down close, and she just grabbed him and held him.

She told him that she loved him, and he said that he loved her too, and later after they left she kept asking for him. It was midnight or one o'clock in the morning, and she just kept saying, "Where's Rhett? Can he come back?" I now wish that I had called them, but it was so late and I just kept telling her that he was asleep and we could call him tomorrow.

Lily's best friend Sophie came over Friday. They had these necklaces, lockets that you could put things in. Sophie had one with an S on it, and Lily had one with an L, but Lily asked to trade, so they did. Lily told Sophie she was her best friend and all this wonderful stuff that only two best girlfriends really appreciate. Sophie will remember that visit for the rest of her life, I'm sure.

## The Babies

Lily was very out of it because of the drugs, going in and out of consciousness. But at one point she said, "I have to get the babies." We didn't know what she meant, and she slipped back into sleep again.

I had chalked it up to delirium from the medication, but then Joey showed me the news article on the shooting at Sandy Hook Elementary. Lily didn't know a thing about it, she couldn't. A deranged gunman had just shot twenty elementary school students and six staff members, killing many of the young students. The "babies"? We would never know.

Just a few hours later, Lily sat up and reached her hands above her, saying, "Mom, Mom!"

"I'm here, I'm right here," I told her.

"I see houses," she told me. "I just need to cross the street...."

Pastor Gibbs and his wife, Debby, were with us, and he gently said, "She is seeing heaven."

She was so close to death, so very, very sick. Heaven was just right there for her. We were very calm, and I just kept rubbing her arm. A couple hours later, she said, "Oh, stop." I asked her what was the matter, and she just said, "I just want to go home."

"Heaven—she wants to go home," Pastor Gibbs said. "She's ready."

I hadn't been sure she would know where to go, and until Pastor Gibbs explained to me, I didn't understand about the houses. She was seeing the mansions Jesus told His disciples about. He had gone ahead of her to prepare a place for her, and she was seeing it through the veil and was so close to both us and eternity that she could tell us about it.

That comforted me greatly. I knew that she would find her way.

Around two o'clock Saturday afternoon, she began making choking noises and couldn't breathe well. Suzanne told me that she was getting very close. So from that time Saturday afternoon until almost midnight, I held her in my arms and did not move. I was so afraid I wouldn't be there when she passed.

Close by, Joey kept softly saying, "It's okay, Lily. It's okay, baby, just go... Go," he softly urged.

If you have never been around someone who is passing away, they make a very unique sound. A sound you will never forget. After fighting for so long, after refusing to quit for three years of brutal treatments, Lily's heart was still strong... But the monster had taken too much of a toll. Her lungs were filling from being in the same position too long and because of the meds.

I was afraid she was choking, but Suzanne told me, "She doesn't know. She's passing...."

We had moved her into the hospice bed, that bed that she didn't want, so that I could lay with her. Joey had his head down on her knees, and he told me, "Jennifer, you are the best Mom ever." We had been through hell together, but he knew that it was different for a mom. I was thankful he understood.

I was staring at our Christmas tree and kept wondering when the miracle would happen. Do angels swoop in and take her? Does she just slip away?

Finally, the battle was over. Lily rattled out her last breath. After so many difficult breaths, after laboring for so long, it was a shock when I was expecting the next one, knew that the next one was coming… And then it didn't. It took a few moments before her pulse faded, and then I finally knew. It was 11:25 p.m., December 15, 2012.

My hero had left this earth to join the ultimate Hero.

# "YES" Till the End

In September 2009, we received news that no family should ever have to hear: "Your child has cancer." From that time until December 15, 2012, the Andersons lived a "YES" life and fought a battle with a horrible monster. Again and again, Lily beat the odds while enduring surgery, chemotherapy, radiation, and more needles, medicines, nurses, and doctors than I can count.

To some, death may seem like the defeat. We choose to think of it like this: Lily lived a "YES" life every day she was on this earth, and she now lives it in heaven! She may have lost her battle with cancer, but she did not lose the war that truly matters—that of the heart.

## With Dignity

Lily had been a hero to so many people, and the community loved her very much. Our local fire department did not want strangers to transport her body. They wanted us to call when she passed, and Joey took care of that. I couldn't move. I held her for a long time even after she had passed.

glitter

Like an honor guard, strong, brave men of our fire department came for my precious girl. The funeral director was there as well, and I remember rattling off conditions to him—don't hurt her, make sure she's warm, and do not take the necklace off her neck! She had a tiny cross, a match for one I wear constantly, that we bought about a year before she died.

That little cross meant a lot to everyone in my family. As a very little girl, I told Lily that God talks to us in a whisper. "You have to be listening at all times," I told Lily and later Audrey. "You've got to listen for the whispers." I told them that God would speak to them and tell them what to do, and these little crosses represented those whispers to us—a little reminder that God is always with us and we should be listening for Him.

We had found these crosses in Neiman Marcus. We were with a friend, Barbara, when Lily saw these necklaces. They were called Whispers, and they were sacred to us as a family! When I saw them, I didn't care if they were $400; we were going to buy them! They were actually only $62, but the significance was far greater than how much we paid for them. Barbara snatched them from Lily's hand and bought them.

I have a matching one, and we wore them all the time. Just a few months before she passed, Lily lost her necklace. In a panic, I called Neiman Marcus, and we got a replacement in September. (The story of where it went is special too, but I will get to that.)

I really impressed on the funeral director in no uncertain terms, "Cannot take that necklace off her neck!" I probably didn't know what I was saying, but then I told him, "It's the only way I'll be able to connect with her. I don't care what you have to do, leave it on!"

He promised that he would, but I wasn't done. I was breaking apart, and raging, I said, "I'm telling you, if I find out you took it off...."

Joey calmed me down, and the firemen wrapped her in a blanket and carried her out like a dignitary. The mortuary had brought their SUV, because I did not want a hearse at my house. They even put in a CD of Lily singing *The Climb* and cranked it! With the fire truck playing her song, the actuary SUV was ready to pull out. People had to hold me up because my legs couldn't do it, and at the last second Joey jumped into the back of the SUV. "I'm going with her!" he said. He rode to the funeral home in the back, holding her while stereo blazed out her songs.

The firefighters also brought their ladder truck, and the 50-foot ladder was illuminated with lime green lights. Ironically, they didn't even know that was Lily's favorite color! Stairway to heaven lit up in her favorite color symbolized that our little girl was meeting Jesus and that the community that loved her was giving her a hero's sendoff.

## When Jesus Comes

The whole time Lily was passing, Audrey was asleep and didn't know what was happening. She had said good-bye to Lily on Saturday afternoon and had gone to play at a friend's house. I don't think she really understood what was happening.

I'm not sure we got any sleep that night, but we brought Audrey into our bed and were altogether when morning came. Joey tackled the difficult task of telling her that her sister had died.

"We've got to tell you something," he told her. "Audrey, you know how sick Lily was, right? Well, she went to heaven last night." Audrey was shocked, stunned. "She went to be with Jesus," Joey went on. "You know how sometimes you're sick and have a tummy ache?" he asked. She said she did. "So, on a scale of one to ten, having a tummy ache is like two. Lily was super sick. You know how sick she was?"

"A ten?" Audrey asked.

"Yes. When you get to ten, Jesus comes to get you, and you go to be with Him."

We told Audrey that it's special to go to heaven and that Lily was all better now! "Can we go too?" she asked.

"No, we can't go there yet. But we're going to go someday," Joey told her. Audrey asked when we could see Lily again, and Joey said, "We don't know, because we don't know when we are going to be a ten. You don't know when Jesus will come to take you to heaven. It's a special thing when you get to go, though."

Audrey was upset that her sister had died, but Joey's amazing way of explaining it to her gave her great peace.

## Ceremonies

Lily touched so many lives, and she lived so fully the years that she had on this earth! It was only right that she had celebrations to match. The viewing before the funeral was four solid hours because the people just lined up. Literally thousands of people had gathered to pay their respects. We were exhausted but amazed to see how many lives she had touched.

On December 19, we had a celebration of Lily's life at our church, Stonecreek, for close friends and family. We asked people to dress Lily style! Casual, cheerful attire, not black, somber funeral clothes. Due to the capacity of the church, we had a second celebration on December 21 at West Forsyth High School for everyone in the community. We didn't want flowers; we asked people to make donations in Lily's name to Children's Healthcare of Atlanta or to St. Jude Hospital. We asked people to bring their lanterns, too!

Lily had touched lives from big to small, including the celebrities she had had a chance to meet. From some singers from Collective Soul, to American Idol performers, she had reached the hearts of so many. Some of them were able to make it for her service!

Very close family and friends came to the service at church, but despite very cold temperatures thousands of people turned out to the high school memorial. The service was at night—I wanted it at night. Because of the lanterns. Everybody brought the lanterns that have become so popular.

Ed Roland and Christopher Alan Yates sang at her service. She had made a huge impression on lead singer Ed Roland, and their song *Shine,* which she had sung with Ed seemingly such a short—yet forever—time ago. It was unbelievably amazing. We had an incredible video of her life and experiences, and then at the end everybody held up a candle, lighting the church's auditorium.

After the ceremony, Joey and I went back to a little room where they had water and snacks and coffee to wait while all the people left. We were going to follow the casket back to the funeral home, but what ended up happening was that we were whisked off to this room while people busily left.

# glitter

All those people lined the street holding thousands of candles and seemed to brighten the night. As we drove out behind the casket, Audrey stood up through the sunroof and waved like a princess to all the people who were there to honor her big sister.

The fire department turned out one of their ladder trucks and lined the 50-foot ladder with lime green lights, Lily's favorite color. It was a stairway to heaven. Many of the firefighters had helped with the annual "Lily's Run," and partly because of my friends on the fire department, they had all fallen in love with her and adopted her.

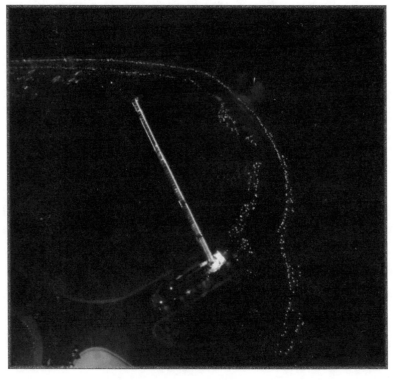

*Around 2,500 people hold candles at Lily's funeral, as the fire truck's green-lit ladder is raised far into the sky in her honor.*

She was a miracle and had touched so many lives. It was so touching to see how the people that she had touched now reached back out to us.

## Love, Jake

We received many letters from people touched by how Lily lived a "YES" life. Many of them go something like this: "I never knew Lily personally, and you don't know me, but when I heard about Lily's fight with cancer, I felt like there was a connection...." They often then go on to say something that changed in their own lives as a result of knowing about Lily and how she lived hers.

Not all of them were strangers though. One young man read his letter to me. His name is Jake Weldy, a boy she had known since second grade. I remember when I first met Jake, so cute and blonde. I asked Lily who he was and she told me his name. When he spoke to me it was always "yes ma'am" and "no ma'am." He was so nice and sweet that I told Lily she was going to go to prom with him! That was in second grade, and I said the same thing in fourth grade. I kept telling Lily she was going to go to prom with Jake until she couldn't handle it anymore! "Mommy, stop with the Jake Weldy stuff!" she would say.

I saw Jake at the visitation. He was crying, and he came up to me to talk. Through my tears, I said, "Jake, you know your job, right?"

"Yes ma'am." I asked him if he knew what it was. "I was going to take Lily to the prom," he said.

I nodded sadly. "I know... I'm really sad that you won't be able to do that. Someday, maybe I can help you find a close second?" I asked.

"Whoever it is, she's going to wear a lily," he told me." A few weeks later, his mom mailed me a letter:

Dear Lily, I hope you never forget me. I'll never forget you! You are my angel. Maybe you can meet my papa while you're in heaven. I know right now you're singing and dancing with the angels. I keep yelling and screaming in my prayers, asking God, why not me—why did it have to be you? I don't understand why He would take away an amazing person like you. I saw Mrs. Jen tonight, and I gave her a big hug—I didn't want to let go. Everybody was surprised that I was crying, but the funny thing is they weren't tears of sadness. They were tears of joy! You are with God and Jesus. You are my light, and because of you I want to be a better Christian. I want to be a leader.
I love you Lily.

—Love, Jake Weldy.

Another little boy named Marc was to be baptized in December. They asked him to tell his story, filming it in November, and he said that he wanted to be baptized because his friend Lily was fighting cancer. Well, they filmed it in November, but he was to be baptized on December 16. Lily died the night before, so he had to get up and go to church and be baptized after his inspiration had just died. But it was actually perfect timing, because the video he recorded in November explaining his inspiration turned out to be the most amazing tribute.

## The King and Queen

Near a mall in our town are two tall buildings called the King and the Queen buildings. They have been there for many years, and every year they light them up for Christmas. With this Christmas, they were different. One was green, but the other one was pink—Lily's favorite colors—all through Thanksgiving and the Christmas season. This was the period where our Lily's condition was really deteriorating. People thought they were lit up just for her.

I tried to figure out if I knew anyone who worked there who would be lighting up a tribute to Lily. It didn't seem like it was anyone I know, but while I was caring for Lily, I didn't have time to look into it. So after she passed, I finally called down there and asked who was responsible for the pink and green lights.

The woman I talked to started laughing when I mentioned the color of the lights, and I asked her what was so funny. She said, "I'm sorry, we've worked hard all holiday season to get them right. It's supposed to be red and green, but they wouldn't go red this year."

I asked, "So you didn't have someone switch them to pink and green for my daughter?"

"No," she said. "What are you talking about?"

I told the woman on the phone all about Lily and her favorite colors, and she said, "I don't believe in coincidences! I promise you, we tried to get red and green for Christmas, but they just won't go red. They keep flickering pink!" She didn't want to hurt my feelings, but she said that it was supposed to be red—they just couldn't keep them from being pink!

In a way, it's a better story because no one requested green and pink. I believe this strongly, and I told the woman so: "That's God... That's just God."

Many people saw these lights, but to me they had a special meaning. But everyone who saw Lily's light was touched by it.

*No one lights a lamp and then puts it under a basket. Instead, a lamp is placed on a stand, where it gives light to everyone in the house. In the same way, let your good deeds shine out for all to see, so that everyone will praise your heavenly Father* (Matthew 5:15-16).

# 1 7

# Whispers

You may remember I told you Lily lost her first Whispers cross necklace. Well, we got her another one, and I was pretty mean to the funeral director and even threatened him! I couldn't handle the thought of them taking it off of her body. We had our precious Lily cremated, but since they cannot cremate jewelry, they took it off just long enough for her to be cremated. Then we put the necklace in with the ashes not an hour after she was cremated.

Time passed, agonizing days of loss and loneliness and grief and sorrow...mixed with sprinklings of joy. But I want to skip ahead to the following Easter. It was April, spring break, and I found myself crying hysterically—at the beach. If you've never done it, it's especially odd to cry at the beach for some reason. But Easter had been a major holiday...and Lily was not with us. I was with Audrey and Joey, and we were trying to enjoy the beach after Easter services, but I was just a mess.

I was digging through my bag for sunscreen for Audrey... when I came across something. I pulled a necklace out of my bag. At first I thought it was mine—that it had broken and fallen in. But my friend who was with us said, "No, that's the necklace Lily lost."

But there is no way she lost it in the beach bag. We had not been to the beach around the time Lily lost her necklace. To this day I do not know how it got there! Yet here we found it, on the day we're celebrating the resurrection.

I immediately knew what it was for. I gave it to Audrey and told her all about why it meant so much to me. I told her about God whispers, and that her big sister had owned that very same necklace. That it was special. She smiled so brightly, brighter than the sunshine there at the beach, and swore, "I'll never take it off!"

Lily no longer needs to have a necklace to remind her to listen for whispers from God. She's there with Him all the time! But Audrey and I find a lot of meaning in having matching necklaces with the one we placed with Lily's ashes.

They remind us to always be listening for gentle whispers from our Lord, and many times I have felt that our little Lily has had a chance to whisper into our lives—not because there's a necklace in her ashes but because we have the same light inside of us she did!

## Beads of Courage

Whenever we went through something difficult at the hospital, Lily received a Bead of Courage. I thought they were pretty cool. If you stay overnight, you get a certain bead. When you get a blood transfusion, you get a bead. When you have surgery, you get a bigger bead. Lose your hair, get a bead.

So Lily accumulated *a lot* of beads in her three-and-a-half years of treatment. I was actually more excited about getting beads when we went to the hospital than Lily was, and I didn't understand why she didn't act excited for a long time.

One day she stopped me from going on about her beads. It was probably a year or six months before she died, so we were pretty far along in her treatments. "Mommy, I don't want the beads."

"Why?" I asked. I didn't understand why she wouldn't want to have something to remember how brave she was.

Her look was far older than her years as she told me, "I don't want to remember every blood transfusion, losing my hair, spending the night in the hospital, or any of it—I *don't want to remember!* I just want to be *normal!*"

This old soul thought differently than every other child. She thought differently than me as well; I enjoyed it, but she thought it was the worst thing ever. I loved how she had processed it and come to her own conclusion.

So I was very torn when I received the worst bead ever—the Butterfly bead. You only get the Butterfly when someone dies. It's the symbol that someone has gotten their wings. No parent wants to get the Butterfly bead, but if you're a parent of a kid who collected Beads of Courage, it's almost like the ultimate final piece of the collection of Courage.

But I didn't know what to do when I received the Butterfly. Should I keep it or throw it in the trash? It was a beautiful glass bead that was a symbol of her life. It was such a struggle, and I finally made the decision…to not make a decision.

My Lily had such a unique perspective. She would get these offers to go on week-long beach vacations from this organization called The Lighthouse. But she didn't want to go on special trips to the beach; she just wanted to be normal.

I think this is just a small example of what made Lily so special. I'm convinced that part of what allowed her to live a "YES" was that she didn't treat her battle with cancer as a reason to feel bad or special. She simply chose to live anyway—to daily say "YES" to normal life, even when she could only have it in her heart.

I pray that I have the strength to say "YES" to life when I could say yes to self-pity, depression, or negativity. I hope that I can live like Lily did just a little bit, every day.

## Lives Lily Touched

Lily had the chance to touch the lives of so many people, ours most of all but including some great celebrities. Scotty McCreery from American Idol met her at a softball game in Nashville, thanks to my brother. She got to meet the runner-up, Lauren Alaina, who grabbed a hold of her and walked her through the crowd, waving. Lauren even drove in from Tennessee for the service. She told me, "Your daughter changed my life. I just drove in from Tennessee because of her, she totally changed my life!"

Her chance to sing with Collective Soul, which she had completely choreographed in her mind before she ever stepped on stage, was the opportunity of a lifetime!

But her favorite was Taylor Swift. Lily had the chance to meet her twice. The first time was when we went to Bridgestone Arena in Nashville. We stood in line for a meet-and-greet, for which we had to wait *thirteen hours!* You had to have a special wristband, which we did not have, but a random girl in the bathroom saw Lily's bald head and bandanna and gave Lily her wristband.

Lily loved Taylor Swift and her music, and she was a very cool person—she seemed to really care. We got to meet her again a year before Lily died because my brother works in Nashville and his wife is with Capital Records. Her dad was a huge DJ in Nashville, and my brother called me and told me to get Lily to Nashville right away so that she could sit in the radio station booth when Taylor Swift walked in on her twenty-first birthday! Lily's hair had grown in by then, and Taylor didn't know she was the same little girl. We got to sit in with her for a two-hour radio interview. Miley Cyrus's song, *The Climb*, was definitely Lily's theme song, and we played it frequently after she passed.

I'd like to think that those two meetings with Lily impacted Taylor's life as well. I've had messages and notes from other celebrities, because Lily did touch their lives. Her light shined brightly, and many saw it!

## It Only Takes One Little Spark

A lot of stars crossed Lily's path, but the thing is, these are just talented people. We can be struck with awe at meeting a celebrity, but my little Lily was a far brighter star than any of them!

We saw her light echoed in the Lanterns for Lily. My Facebook page was literally filled with pictures of people from across the country and as far away as Australia lighting their own small lights to commemorate our little light.

Lanterns for Lily was the result of Lily's loving cheerleading coach, April, who wrote some kind words to me that I would like to share.

I met Lily in the fall of 2009. It was my first year as a cheerleading coach, and she was the honorary homecoming queen for our third grade football team. Lily had already been diagnosed with neuroblastoma and was undergoing chemotherapy. She was losing her hair and wore a wig. The Andersons didn't want too many people talking to her in order to limit germ exposure. Other than her wig, you would not know she was going through treatment. She had an inner glow and looked radiant.

Lily cheered with my teams for three years. I never knew Lily without the cancer. But Lily never let cancer define who she was—an amazing girl. She always had a smile on her face when she saw someone and always had a hug ready.

Don't get me wrong, Lily hated having cancer and sometimes hated what she could and could not do because of it. The first few years Lily was a flyer (the girl who gets lifted up by others), but the last year her legs were in too much pain. She'd still give me those eye rolls that every kid does, and say, "Coach April! I want to go up." I hated saying no to Lily, so my co-coach, Jamie Garfield, and I would lift her up so she could fly and to keep her safe. (Shhh, don't tell Jen!)

But Lily never let cancer get the best of her. Even during her final cheerleading season when she was unable to walk, she proudly stayed on the sidelines and cheered as a member of our squad. I admired her and respected her for never giving up. She was an awesome cheerleader and I loved having her on my squads. I learned more from her than she ever did from me.

When Lily's cancer returned, I was heartbroken. I wasn't sure what to do for her so I did the only thing I could. I got on my knees to pray. I prayed intensely for Lily. I believed in God, but I didn't go to church and wasn't always faithful in my beliefs. I admit I struggled with questions of faith. "How could a good God do this to a child? Why Lily?" I am still struggling with questions, but I do know that God is there. And Lily's mom, Jen, was the one who made me start listening to Him. There were little things that happened. Praying for Lily in my car one day, I turned up the radio and heard a song by my favorite college band, which I'd never heard before—on a station I normally don't listen to—titled *"Lily"*! Another time, calamine lotion spilled in a drawer and formed a perfect pink ribbon after I prayed. Jen calls those little events "God whispers"!

A big whisper came in early October 2012 when I heard a father on the radio telling the story of his son's parachuting accident. His son's name was John and he was named after his grandfather and father, thus he was John III. John had to go through several surgeries but had made a miraculous recovery. His dad was explaining how he felt that God had a presence in their lives the whole time from the moment they assigned John to his room, 316.[3] The dad stayed at the hospital until he knew that his son was going to be all right. The first time John's dad left the hospital, he prayed to God and thanked Him for saving his son. Right at that moment, a car pulled out in front of him with the license plate "LUV J3." J3 was John's parachuting call name! He was so stunned that he whipped out his camera phone and took a picture of it. The radio posted the picture. The love of John's dad was so profound that the story really stuck with me.

A few weeks later my cheerleading squad, family, and members of the community and beyond participated in "Lily's Run." That Sunday morning, I got down on my knees and prayed. Lily had been very sick, and they weren't even sure that she would feel well enough to leave the house and attend. I prayed that Lily would be able to come to the race. I was still struggling with questions concerning my faith, and I asked God, "I wonder if You would ever show me a sign so that I know You are listening? Something that bonks me upside the head and I wouldn't question?" A few hours later, as my family made the turn into "Lily's Run," the car in front of us had "LILIANA" on the plate! I screamed so loud my husband almost ran off the road! I took a picture of the license plate. When I first read it, I thought perhaps it could mean "God gives Lili an

---

[3] John 3:16 is one of the most widely quoted verses from the Christian Bible. *"For God so loved the world, that he gave his only begotten Son, that whosoever believeth in him should not perish, but have everlasting life"* (KJV).

A," but later I found out that Lily's given name is Lilian A(nderson) – LILIANA!

A few months later, around Thanksgiving, we knew Lily wasn't doing well. Over the past few weeks, I had been hearing a phrase from a song in my head – *"It only takes a spark to get a fire going...."* I knew it meant something but couldn't figure out what. I kept hearing just that part, and it's the only part I could remember. I did recall that I used to sing it when I was a little girl at church and at camp.

During a visit to a friend's house, we were brainstorming what we could do to show Jen we were there for her. We knew there wasn't anything we could do to make Lily better, but we wanted a way to show Jen and Lily that we did love and support them. We tossed around ideas like leaving them inspirational notes or lighting a candle each night. Once I got home, it hit me—*Lanterns for Lily*. My neighbor and I decided to light eleven lanterns (Lily's age) and have a different family/group deliver them to their house each night. Once I was home that night, I sent an e-mail to a few friends to get the word out for signing up. I also made a Facebook page for other people to light lanterns in their own driveways in honor of Lily.

Lanterns for Lily spread throughout our community and across the country in just five short days! We used eleven white or pink and green (which were Lily's favorite colors) bags or even decorated mason jars and lit them each night until Christmas. It spread because everyone loved Lily, and we all wanted to do something to show it. But it's also because "God knew way before we did that she would impact the world and touch thousands of lives," as Jen said. Jen sent out an e-mail asking everyone to light the eleven lanterns not just for Lily, but to raise awareness for childhood cancer. A friend said, "In typical Jen fashion, she has taken a loving gesture for her family and made it into something bigger for others!"

As for the lyrics to the song I couldn't get out of my head, talking about it only taking one spark to get a fire going. It talks about experiencing God's love and passing it on.

I honestly believe that Lily came into this world to pass the light of God to the rest of us. Lily is now in heaven. She always said, "I want to be the flyer, Coach April"…and now I know that she is flying with the angels. Because of Lily, I have now gotten back on my knees to pray; and because of Jen, I now listen for God's whispers. Attending Lily's "Celebration of Life" service was perfect! It was beautiful and one of the most spiritual events I've ever attended. My heart hurts every day for Jen, but I know she will see her sweet angel, Lily, when God decides it's time. I try to live a "YES" for Lily, and I have promised to continue shining Lily's light through me.

I received so many notes and letters a lot like this—people sharing the light that Lily's glittering life reflected into their own lives! I want to share one more with you out of the hundreds I received because I feel it so perfectly represents the amazing reach that Lily's life had—and the power of living a "YES!"

# Sisterhood of the Traveling Bracelet

I never had the privilege of meeting Lily in person before she passed away, but I believe I was the very lucky recipient of a "Lily Whisper."

The whisper happened during a time when I was struggling with uncharacteristic negativity, and some sweet friends who knew Lily shared the idea of living a "YES" life. They talked about Lily's amazing grace, grit, wit, and wisdom beyond her years. They shared stories of how she was able to brighten any room into which she walked and how she faced her circumstances with such determination to live that "YES" life. This resonated deeply with me, and I was inspired and determined to shed the negativity.

One morning, I was having coffee with a close friend, Kristan, and she told me about a project she was working on with her staff. The project was based on a book called *The Power of One*. Briefly, you choose a word, which will be your anchor for a year. Her staff was going to make a collage including each of their words to support and encourage each other throughout the year. Before she could finish her description, I interrupted and told her that I knew, without question, that my word would be "YES"!

Kristan got teary-eyed and said, "I have something for you." She pulled a beaded bracelet out of her purse that said, *"Say Yes."* She went on to explain that a teacher at her school had stopped her in the hall nearly three weeks earlier and handed her the bracelet. She had told Kristan that she didn't know exactly why she made it, or who it was for, but she was certain that she was supposed to give it to Kristan.

I carry the bracelet in my purse as a reminder to continue living a "YES" life, and I listen for a "Whisper" to know when it is time to pass the bracelet on to another lucky recipient.

Thank you, Lily, for living a "Yes!"

Amy Rodriguez

# 1 8

# Will You Live a "YES"?

Lily was my best friend. I know you're not supposed to be best friends with your daughter, but she was mine. We just got it. We really had something that most mommies and their daughters don't have. I see so many moms who fight with their daughters, and I know how special what I had with Lily really was. She told me everything.

She was always able to make others feel special, important. One little boy shared with me how he had been bullied and picked on in school but that Lily had always made him feel good about himself. That was lowly—she had her close friends, she was a friend to everyone. She really embraced something Joey told her: "It's okay if you don't like everyone, but you've got to love everyone."

When she was having trouble in school, he also wrote a quote on her bathroom mirror that is still there today: "Watch your thoughts, they become your words. Watch your words, they become your actions. Watch your actions, they become habits. Watch your habits, they become your character. Watch your character, it becomes your destiny."

She did that, and so much more. She really embodied what living a "YES" life is all about.

I want to share that message with others, because it's important to understand that no matter what you've been through, it's not over. I lost the biggest thing in my life. Losing a child is not even comprehensible—it's not supposed to be. You may try, but you just can't wrap your mind around it.

But you have to get up the next day. You have to go forward, you have to take another step no matter how hard you fall.

Right after Lily died, I felt like I couldn't move. It was an almost impossible effort just to get up out of bed, just to take a shower, just to make lunch. Even something simple like getting to the bank felt like too much to handle. I couldn't make it to the gym or do other things that I knew would be good for me—they were just too much.

But I *had* to get back up. I had to *live* again!

I knew it's what Lily would want.

I don't know what you've been through. You may have lost someone dear to you or have endured some other great tragedy. Believe it or not, the point isn't about what has happened to you. The point is what you are going to do *next*.

Will you stay down? Will you let life beat you? Or will you choose to live a "YES" life?

There is no one secret, a silver bullet that will work for all of us. Living a "YES" is about one choice after another, getting up one day after another, living one day at a time.

I learned that the thing about the "YES" life is that it's not enough to have seen it lived or heard about it; you have to continue living it yourself.

## Will You Live a "YES"?

Pastor Steven Gibbs' speech at Lily's service was all about how she had lived a "YES" life in that we all need to make a daily choice to say "YES" to life too. He spoke so movingly about how Lily smiled constantly and made such a difference in people's lives. He shared how she told people they had a purpose, that there was a reason for everything that happened.

She would say that even about her death.

She shared that incredible insight that she had at the tender age of eleven: that we should not cry over her death as though she were lost. "Don't let the devil win," she would urge us if she were alive.

Pastor Gibbs challenged us to not let those tears go to waste and to answer a question for ourselves, and I want to share some of his thoughts on what we are to do with our tears.

I don't usually ask the question "why." People say, "Don't you want to know why?" We usually do—we want to understand. But I have this deep-seated conviction about the world that we live in. Yes, these things happen—bad things happen, and Lily's passing is one of the worst I have personally been near. This world is not fully as it was intended to be, and events happen in this life that we can never understand. But God is not the cause of these bad things—this I know.

In fact, I have complete certainty that God is good, and He will be God, even in the middle of the worst situations. He promises that He will work it out for our *good*. With these convictions, what's important isn't "*why*"—it's how we choose to *respond* to these situations. How do we handle tragedy? How do we handle loss, questions of faith, and troubles of all kinds?

See, we can cry a lot of tears, ask "why" and rage against the world in which we live—a world that has words like "neuroblastoma" in it and that steals away little girls only beginning to live. But if we don't *do* something, if we don't let these loses *impact us*, our tragedies haven't really changed us. If we don't do something, then our tears are empty. If we don't make changes to how we live, our tears are about us, not about Lily.

What needs to change? Instead of asking "why," instead of just crying, we have a choice to make: We must choose to live a "YES!"

Jennifer's story about Lily catching her crying shows that Lily knew something about life—if you just sit and cry, the devil wins. That's big girl stuff. We see in her life Lily's response to the harshness of this life. Yes, she cried when it hurt—we all do. *But she didn't stop there.* With the help of family and support, even through the pain Lily lived a "YES."

She could do that because of the light Jesus shined into her life.

I think one aspect of Jesus' light that He planted deep in Lily's life was this: No matter what life threw her way, she lived a "YES" so that her light would shine brightly for us to see. She did not stop going; she kept on moving. Even when most of us would have laid down and quit, Lily didn't. For her it was about *the climb*, the title of her favorite song.

The light that Lily shined was the light that Jesus shined through her. Make no mistake—Lily was wonderful, and she was so beautiful and had a great smile. She brought all of us joy. But Lily wasn't perfect—Jesus *in her* was perfect. Only Jesus is able to give a light to be shined, and His light was so present in Lily. And everyone around her could see it.

Because of Jesus' light in Lily, we too can live a "YES" as she did. We can experience that same impact and can have the same future hope. We can share a future that words can't even begin to describe that Lily is already experiencing and glimpsed before she died.

One thing she is experiencing is that she has a new home. In fact, we all will receive a new home. Jesus says this: *"Let not your heart be troubled; you believe in God, believe also in Me. In My Father's house are many mansions; if it were not so, I would have told you. I go to prepare a place for you. And if I go and prepare a place for you, I will come again and receive you to Myself; that where I am, there you may be also. And where I go you know, and the way you know."*[4]

---

[4] John 14:1-4 NKJV.

Jesus has gone to prepare a place for us, and even though we can't go now, we will go there when we follow Him. We can read some descriptions of what heaven looks like in the Bible, and one stands out: *"Look! Look! God has moved into the neighborhood, making his home with men and women! They're his people, he's their God. He'll wipe every tear from their eyes. Death is gone for good—tears gone, crying gone, pain gone—all the first order of things gone... Look! I'm making everything new...."*[5]

So here we have a brief description of what heaven will be like. But the real point of heaven is that God is there. It's like real estate. Some of you know the three most important things in real estate: location, location, location. What makes for a good location? If God is there, it's a good location.

When she went to her new home, God was waiting for Lily. Over the course of Friday and Saturday as she passed, Lily mentioned "crossing the street"—she was going home. We may know nice neighborhoods with beautiful trees, great shops, and terrific neighbors, but no neighborhood here on earth can hold a candle to heaven. None of them are really *home!*

For Lily's memorial, beautiful lanterns lined the drive leading up to the church. But imagine how much more beautiful the streets of gold that Lily crossed are! She crossed those streets of gold and went home.

---

[5] Revelation 21:3-5 MSG.

Lily got a new home, and we can too—if we live a "YES" for Jesus.

Lily also got a new body. For those of us who are aging, I think our new bodies will be like this: About age twenty-seven, body fat 7.5 percent, waist size what it was in high school, straight teeth, and no gray hair—or hairless heads unless you like that—no wrinkles. That's the resurrection body I'm praying for, at least!

What we do know is that it will be indestructible, won't wear out, and won't grow old. No sickness or disease, no signs of aging, no over or underweight. It won't be ravaged by cancer or tumors. It won't need chemotherapy or surgery or stem cell transplants or antibody therapy or radiation. It won't suffer from low platelets or having its hair fall out. It will be a restored body. We will all get a perfect new body that will accomplish the purpose God intends for us. Lily has a new body that's glorious in its beauty and perfection.

Speaking of this day when we will all be with God in heaven, one of Jesus' friends writes: *Then the righteous will shine like the sun in the kingdom of their Father....*[6] If you thought Lily shined brightly on earth, can you imagine Lily in heaven, shining like the sun? We will all shine like the sun shines—vibrant and brilliant and breathtaking.

Lily is shining like none of us have ever experienced—but not only that, she is at *rest*. Not a rest like taking a nap,

---

[6] Matthew 13:43 NIV.

but rest as in enjoying having accomplished a goal. She finished her race, and now she gets to rest. She's not fighting anymore. She has rest, for she is not worrying anymore. Lily hadn't rested in over three years, and neither did her family. While there were good days, she didn't get the opportunity to rest. But now she's resting.

She got a new body, and we can too—if we live a "YES."

We also get a new name in heaven. I love thinking about what that name will be. In the Bible, names carry special meaning. It's more than an identifier that we're called by; it carries meaning about who we are and what our created purpose in life is. The Bible teaches that each of us is created with a purpose, and we will have a name that communicates that purpose. Only God knows that name, and we will learn it when we cross over into heaven.

Right now, we live in a fallen world, and we can hear but echoes of our heavenly names. But eventually, we will hear clearly and see clearly.[7] We called Lily by many names— Lily, Lilian, Sissy, and others. But we also had names for her based on her and who she was, her effect on this world, and what she liked to do on this earth.

I think we can imagine aspects of Lily's life that hinted at her new name. Her smile, of course, needs to be part of it her new name. Her smile endured through sickness and treatments and adversity, and I think that it will be part of what God uses to name her. I think another aspect of her

---

[7] 1 Corinthians 13:12.

new name will be her *fight*, which some might call a stubborn streak. Even in her last hours, she was the ultimate fighter. That's something all of us could take a lesson on: *She. Would. Not. Give. Up!* She had a glimmer in her eyes that always said "YES!" Her eyes shined like the sun, inviting and warm and so full of life. They had a way of capturing you and not letting go, sticking with you.

As I got to know the Andersons, Lily would run down the hallway to me as I walked toward the church lobby and jump up into my arms. She gave the best hugs! Her parents would try to get her to leave me alone, reminding her that I had other people to speak to. But I felt like Jesus when He told His disciples not to turn away the little children because the Kingdom of Heaven belonged to those who are like little children.[8] He got down to the children's level, so I know that Lily is now doing with Jesus what she did in our church lobby—jumping up and giving (and receiving) the best hugs imaginable!

I can just imagine Lily's smile for Him as she finished the climb and crossed the street to the other side, from this life to eternity. Jesus called her by a new name, and she entered her new home. I can only imagine the warmth she felt in her heart, the strength she immediately felt in her new, perfect body, and the joy that she felt rise from the depths of her soul with the hope that we here alive on earth hold so dearly.

Lily got a new name, and we can too—if we live a "YES."

---

[8] Matthew 19:14.

So what do we learn from all this? Where do we go from here? No matter how old you are—student, young adult, parent, or grandparent. No matter who you are—mom, dad, cheerleader, firefighter, coach, or rock star. You have a lesson to learn, and lives around you are just waiting to be changed as Lily changed ours.

For many of us, Lily can become a fleeting memory, and the real tragedy may not even be her death—it would be that we hadn't learned anything from her life. The tragedy may be that we keep on as we have, with our lives unaffected by the light we saw reflected in Lily. As the days and weeks go by after you finish reading this book, you can begin to forget the "YES" life you've heard about.

My hope is that as we celebrate the "YES" life that Lily showed us, we are challenged enough by it to *live it ourselves*. My challenge to you, now that you have read this book and seen the impact one little girl can have, is that you will commit to living a "YES" in your own life.

The only way your light can continue to burn and your life can matter is by understanding that Jesus came to give you life that will last forever. If you choose to live a "YES."

Lily's life verse was Matthew 5:15, which says, *"No one lights a lamp and then puts it under a basket. Instead, a lamp is placed on a stand, where it gives light to everyone in the house."* The next verse goes on to say, *"In the same way, let your good deeds shine out for all to see, so that everyone will praise your heavenly Father."*

"Let your light shine," it says. Jesus is the Light of the World. The light that shines in us is the light that God shines *through* us. This light is what allows us to live a "YES."

Lily lived a "YES." She's still living a "YES."

The temptation when things get hard is to stop trying, but if we learned nothing else from Lily, we must learn to never stop saying "YES" to life. There will always be another mountain to climb, and we've got to keep our heads up.

Lily and her family faced mountains like few of us will ever endure. When she was in her final days, Jen asked me some hard questions. "Did it work? Did three-and-a-half years of hospital visits and chemo treatments and platelets and blood transfusions and needles work?"

I had to answer her honestly: "It depends." It depends on where we go from here. If all Lily did was make us sad, it didn't work. But if the fight of this little girl inspires us to keep going and keep living until we too go to see our Maker, then it worked.

If you finish reading this book with a greater appreciation for your life and a stronger sense of responsibility to do something—to live a "YES"—then it worked. I will count it an honor for the rest of my life to have been present, together with my wife and the Andersons, as Lily made her final journey home. When I look back at it now, I don't see the suffering. I think Lily showed us in her last hours the most important thing she could have showed us.

She showed us how to live, and die, with a "YES" to our God. She showed us how to live with a heart so big that no matter what kind of fight life brings us, we will hit it head-on with a "YES." Lily did not back down. Ever. She gave it everything she had.

Did it work? We all have to answer that question for ourselves—and keep answering every day we live from here forward.

Will you live a "YES"?

—Pastor Steven Gibbs, Stonecreek Church

# 1 9

# My Dream of Lily

There is no way to perfectly describe losing a child. It defies words. I don't want anyone to even *try* to imagine it, because the pain is so deep. It's suffocating... You just want to stop the bleeding, the hurt, the yearning. I oftentimes feel like I don't even see color anymore. I just live in this hazy world of muted tones.

But some days... Some days a speck of color confronts you, and it's *magnificent*. You just want to believe that it is your loved one coming through to push you through another moment in this life here on earth.

I had an amazing dream of Lily in March 2013. It was my brother Shane's birthday—Shane and Lily had a very special relationship, so I am not surprised that she picked that day to come into my dreams, a bright little speck of color.

Lily was dressed in a flowing white top almost too big for her tiny frame and her navy skinny jeans. She always had this slight pigeon-toed stance, and she stood in front of me with her dainty sandals and crooked feet. I was sitting on a bench, but she filled my vision—I could see nothing else. A thick fog surrounded me, and I reached out to grab her, gasping for breath.

I held her close, my head buried against her chest as she stood in front of me and I sat on the bench. I kissed her and squeezed her tight.

"*Are you okay? Lily, are you okay?*" After I'd asked about twenty-five times, Lily, in her oh-so-calm and composed way, looked at me and said, "Yeah, Mom, I'm fine."

Her smile was as big as life. She was perfect—healthy and happy.

Seconds later, I sat up in bed, crying. It was a dream…. I was so upset, I quickly closed my eyes and tried to fall back to sleep so I could see her and kiss her and hold her again. But she was gone…again.

The tears flowed, but they were bittersweet. If only in my dreams, if only for one brief moment, I had held my Lily again and experienced vivid color.

## The Fight Goes On

Time passes, and the tears come less frequently—most of the time. I often wonder what she would look like today. I would give anything to hear her voice, to see her smile, or to spoon with her again, safe and snuggled in bed.

Lily left us a legacy, and everyone around us lives a YES because of her. I truly believe that Lily was sent here to earth with a purpose. She was sent to make a change, and she did just that. She has changed an entire community of people. Her presence made a difference, and I am proud to be the one chosen to be her mom.

The time we were blessed to share with Lily on this earth left us all with a higher calling—not just to survive, but to say YES to *really living*. Every day is a gift. Health itself is a gift.

## One Last "YES" Story

One day Lily and I were eating dinner after a long day at the hospital having chemo. She looked across the dining room and spotted a family celebrating a birthday. It was a teenage girl, and we both giggled, saying that it was probably the girl's sixteenth birthday! She was probably going to get a car! Lily *dreamed* of being sixteen. She had told Joey that she wanted a Pink jeep for her Sweet Sixteen.

So guessing it was this girl's Sweet Sixteen, Lily practically begged me to surprise the birthday girl with a piece of chocolate cake! But Lily didn't want them to know it was from us…. She wanted me to pay for the cake and ask our waiter to deliver it *after* we had left. So I did!

Lily was brave enough to stop at the table and say "happy birthday" in a sweet little voice as we left. The girl looked at Lily and just smiled and thanked her so much. Lily ventured to ask, "Are you sixteen?" and the girl smiled again. "YES!" she exclaimed!

Then her mom said, "We are celebrating Lily's sixteenth birthday!" We both just stopped breathing for a second.

"Did you say your name is Lily?" I asked.

She nodded. "Yes," she said.

I could not believe it.... Of all the names and all the people in the world, the girls had the SAME NAME!

We talked for a moment and then walked out of the restaurant feeling satisfied that we would change her day in just moments with the incredible chocolate cake! Lily and I even waited in the car and tried to peek in the window, but it was impossible to see. We pulled away knowing that we may never cross paths again but that the "Lily" turning sixteen would remember her special cake forever.

*Lily surprised this "Lily" with a piece of chocolate cake for her sixteenth birthday.*

Well, a few days later I posted the story on Carepages.com, and someone who knew someone who knew someone recognized the story from their friends, whose daughter had turned sixteen at P. F. Chang's! The family sent me a note asking to meet again. They said that our Lily had changed their Lily's life....

They were so surprised at the cake from a little girl who was fighting for her life.

The girls got to meet again at "Lily's Run" 2011, and it was the most amazing reunion. It was like they had known each other for years.

Lily was living a YES before we even knew that would be her legacy.

My hope is that in reading this book you might choose to let Lily's life inspire you and encourage you to live a YES yourself. Maybe you'll feel like changing some things about your own life—or how you view life itself. Maybe you'll decide to give of your time and volunteer or give financially to help a good cause. Maybe you'll donate blood plasma, or take other steps that help save lives. Maybe you'll decide that it's time to take better care of yourself and your own health so you'll be there for your children and grandchildren.

Maybe you'll give a piece of chocolate cake and change a life, like Lily did.

Whatever reading Lily's story may do for you, I pray that it gives you the power to *live a YES!*

glitter

*Lily at the finish line of "Lily's Run" 2012.*

# ABOUT THE AUTHOR

Jennifer Anderson was born in Rochester, Minnesota, but moved to Pittsburgh, Pennsylvania, as a young child with her parents and three siblings. She attended the University of Pittsburgh where she earned her degree in communication science in 1993. After graduation Jennifer moved to Atlanta for a summer, and discovering all that it had to offer, she decided to stay. In 1996 she became licensed in real estate, and has been successfully selling it ever since.

In 2000 Jennifer married her husband, Joey. Lily was their first bundle of joy, born in May 2001, followed by her sister, Audrey, in February 2007. Currently, Jennifer is trying to be the best Mom she can be for Audrey, Joey owns a custom cabinetry business, and they live in Atlanta, Georgia.

Jennifer never thought she'd write a book, but she's proud of Lily and her journey, and proud of Audrey for having been the best little sister to Lily and an amazing daughter! She's learning to breathe with a mending heart, and while she and Lily wait to be reunited someday, she clings to the verse, *"But do not forget this one thing, dear friends: With the Lord a day is like a thousand years, and a thousand years are like a day"* (2 Peter 3:8 NIV).

If you would like to contact Jennifer, find out more information, purchase books, or request Jennifer to speak, please contact:

Jennifer Anderson
janderson526@bellsouth.net
www.LillianKateAnderson.com

Top - Delaney Ward, Lyndsey Bowers, Lily, Hailey Bowers, Audrey Anderson

Middle - Gina Blakely, Lily, Adam Blakely

Bottom - Kamryn Spivia, Kellie Pickler, Lily

Top - Lily, Matt Kabus

Middle - Grandma Anderson,
Audrey Anderson, Lily

Bottom - Taylor Swift, Lily

Top - Front Row: Delaney Schumate,
Brynlee Fife, Kyleigh Grosvenor, Lily,
Kristen Sorrell, Emma Claire Russell
Back Row: Haleigh Miller, Emily Matson,
Sophie Sutphin, Emma Cole,
Hayley Makowski, Zoe Taddeo,
Kaitlin Reed, Virginia Kennedy

Middle - Lauren Alaina, Lily

Bottom - Lily, Hannah Sklenka

Top - Front Row: Emma Claire
Russell, Lily
Back Row: Marlene "Nana"
Tallant, Mike "Pop Pop" Tallant

Middle - Kylie Beal, Lily

Bottom - Lily, Scotty McCreery

Top - Lily, Kyleigh Grosvenor

Middle - Lily, Brian McCann

Bottom - Lily, Ed Roland

Top - Jennifer Anderson,
Debbie Kalb, Lily, Charlie Kalb

Middle - Lily, Steven Gibbs,
Debby Gibbs

Bottom - Jack Hodges, Lily

*Top left - Lily, Annie Keller*

*Top right - Lily, Delaney Schumate*

*Bottom left - Lily, Rhett Williams*

*Bottom right - Lily*